A PARALLEL PRESS CHAPBOOK

AMERICA'S FOUNDERS

THOMAS JEFFERSON

Philosopher and Politician

JOHN P. KAMINSKI

PARALLEL PRESS · 2005

ISBN 1-893311-59-7

America's Founders is a chapbook series published by Parallel Press, an imprint of the University of Wisconsin–Madison Libraries, in collaboration with the Center for the Study of the American Constitution, in the Department of History at the University of Wisconsin–Madison.

http://parallelpress.library.wisc.edu

FIRST EDITION

The America's Founders series is dedicated to the several hundred Mentor Teachers who are the heart and soul of the Center for Civic Education's program "We the People: The Citizen and the Constitution."

This chapbook is dedicated to
DAVID RICHMOND
Centennial High School
Bakersfield, California
&
ROGER DESROSIERS
Millbury Memorial Junior/Senior High School
Millbury, Massachusetts

AMERICA HAS BEEN BLESSED WITH FEW RENNAISANCE MEN. Certainly Thomas Jefferson is among this group—some would argue that only he and Benjamin Franklin fall into this category. Among his many accomplishments, Jefferson was a statesman, parliamentarian, codifier of laws, antiquarian, historian, surveyor, philosopher, diplomat, scientist, architect, inventor, educator, lawyer, farmer, breeder, manufacturer, botanist, horticulturist, anthropologist, archaeologist, meteorologist, paleontologist, lexicologist, linguist, ethnologist, biblicist, mathematician, astronomer, geographer, librarian, bibliophile, bibliographer, classicist, scholar and historian of religions, cryptographer, translator, writer, editor, musician, and gastronome and connoisseur of wine.

Jefferson's skill as a writer has accentuated many of his accomplishments. Partly because of his preference for style over a rigid adherence to the rules of grammar, he was perhaps the most eloquent of all American writers. Congressman John Adams, in identifying the thirty-three-year-old Virginian as the person who should write the Declaration of Independence, said that Jefferson had "a masterly Pen" and "a remarkable felicity of expression."

More than most of the Founders, Thomas Jefferson is hard to understand, even paradoxical, not only for us today, but also for the people of his own time. Though he was far more the theoretical philosopher than his contemporaries, he incessantly left the safety and seclusion of his mountaintop retreat to brave the violence and turbulence of revolution and diplomacy, of partisan politics and public service. He served almost continuously, though sometimes reluctantly, in the colonial and state legislatures, the

Continental and Confederation congresses, as governor of Virginia, minister to France, secretary of state, political party leader, and as the second vice president and third president of the United States. Jefferson not only wrote the words of the Declaration of Independence, but he thoroughly believed in the revolutionary principles they espoused and consistently attempted to implement those principles in the real world of practical politics.

As a political philosopher, Jefferson was greatly admired and savagely condemned by his contemporaries. Jefferson's political enemies (as well as some later historians) belittled him "as a man of sublimated & paradoxical imagination—cherishing notions incompatible with regular and firm government."[1] Alexander Hamilton saw Jefferson's politics as "tinctured with fanaticism," and believed that he was "too much in earnest in his democracy."[2] Even after Jefferson's first administration, perhaps the most successful term of any American president, skeptics remained. New Hampshire Senator William Plumer described President Jefferson as

> a man of science. . . . he knows little of the nature of man—very little indeed. . . . He has much knowledge of books—of insects—of shells & of all that charms a virtuoso—but he knows not the human heart. He is a closet politician—but not a practical statesman. He has much *fine sense* but little of that *plain common sense* so requisite to business—& which in fact governs the world.[3]

Some detractors saw Jefferson's posture as the detached philosopher as a ruse of "A man of profound ambition &

1. Alexander Hamilton to John Steele, Philadelphia, October 15, 1792, Harold C. Syrett, ed., *The Papers of Alexander Hamilton* (27 vols., New York, 1961-1987), XII, 569.

2. To James A. Bayard, New York, January 16, 1801, ibid., XXV, 319.

3. William Plumer Memorandum, March 16, 1806, Everett Somerville Brown, ed., *William Plumer's Memorandum of Proceedings in the Senate, 1803–1807* (New York, 1923).

violent passions."[4] The gossipy John Nicholas, clerk of Jefferson's Albemarle County, told George Washington that Jefferson was "one of the most artful, intriguing, industrious and double-faced politicians in all America."[5]

Admirers, however, like James Madison could readily forgive Jefferson's sometimes impractical ideas because they so admired his commitment to republican principles and his remarkable ability to express those principles with an eloquence that approached poetry. It seemed to Margaret Bayard Smith, the matriarch of Washington society, "impossible, for any one personally to know him & remain his enemy."[6]

Jefferson believed that every man owed his country "a debt of service . . . proportioned to the bounties which nature & fortune have measured to him."[7] Some men were "born for the public. Nature, by fitting them for the service of the human race on a broad scale, has stamped them with the evidences of her destination & their duty."[8] The Revolutionary generation, Jefferson believed, had been "thrown into times of a peculiar character, and to work our way through them has required services & sacrifices from our countrymen generally, and, to their great honor, these have been generally exhibited, by every one in his sphere, & according to the opportunities afforded."[9]

Jefferson was convinced that he was "conscientiously called" to his "tour of duty" and was confident that he faith-

4. Alexander Hamilton to Edward Carrington, Philadelphia, May 26, 1792, *Hamilton Papers*, XI, 444.

5. February 22, 1798, Donald Jackson et al., eds., *The Papers of George Washington* (Charlottesville, Va., 1976-), Ret. Ser., II, 101.

6. Smith's account of her visit to Monticello, J. Jefferson Looney, ed., *The Papers of Thomas Jefferson* (Retirement Series, Princeton, 2004), I, 393.

7. To Edward Rutledge, Monticello, December 27, 1796, Julian P. Boyd et al., eds., *The Papers of Thomas Jefferson* (Princeton, 1950-), XXIX, 233.

8. To James Monroe, Washington, January 13, 1803, Merrill D. Peterson, ed., *Thomas Jefferson: Writings* (New York, 1984), 1112.

9. To James Fishback, Monticello, September 27, 1809, Looney, *Jefferson*, I, 565.

fully responded.[10] His "affections were first for my own country, and then generally for all mankind."[11] Jefferson was a revolutionary who welcomed change, with one exception: "the inherent and unalienable rights of man" were unchangeable and needed constant vigilance to protect.[12] To protect these rights, Jefferson made difficult decisions that sometimes meant choosing "a great evil in order to ward off a greater."[13] But throughout his life his guiding principle was "to do whatever is right, and leave consequences to him who has the disposal of them."[14] He hoped that his contemporaries and posterity would understand. "The only exact testimony of a man is his actions, leaving the reader to pronounce on them his own judgment."[15]

· · · · ·

This chapbook is dedicated to David Richmond of Centennial High School in Bakersfield, California, and to Roger Desrosiers of Millbury Memorial Junior/Senior High School in Millbury, Massachusetts—two of the great mentor teachers associated with the Center for Civic Education. Dave and Roger are vastly different kinds of people and teachers. Dave, a born leader, is the extrovert, who will do anything—including embarrassing himself—to get his point across. Roger, much more the introvert, is thoughtful and caring. Dave prods his students; Roger nurtures them. Both are totally devoted to their students and to the subject matter. They are extraordinary teachers. I admire and have learned from them.

10. Jefferson to Horatio Gates, Monticello, February 3, 1794, and to Ferdinando Fairfax, Monticello, April 25, 1794, *Jefferson Papers*, XXVIII, 14, 58.

11. To Thomas Law, Monticello, January 15, 1811, H.A. Washington, ed., *The Writings of Thomas Jefferson* (9 vols., Washington, D.C., 1853–1854), V, 556.

12. To John Cartwright, Monticello, June 5, 1824, *Jefferson: Writings*, 1494.

13. To William Short, Monticello, November 28, 1814, ibid., 1356.

14. To George Logan, Monticello, October 3, 1813, Washington, *Jefferson: Writings* VI, 217.

15. To Louis H. Girardin, Monticello, March 27, 1815, ibid., 455.

Early Life

Born on April 13, 1743, on the fringe of the Virginia frontier, Thomas Jefferson was the eldest of seven children—five girls and two boys. Jefferson's father, Peter, was a prosperous, self-made Albemarle County planter/surveyor. His marriage to Jane Randolph, the daughter of a wealthy planter from a distinguished family, not only assisted Peter financially, but contributed to his rise socially and politically. Peter, a vestryman in his local Anglican congregation, served Albemarle County as a colonel in the militia, sheriff, justice of the peace, and burgess in Virginia's colonial legislature.

Young Thomas Jefferson was truly shaped by his times. He was raised and imbued with the spirit of the Enlightenment, which recognized the perfectibility of both man and government through education and the discovery of well-designed natural laws using man's innate reason. Although always an optimist, Jefferson's immersion in the Whig political writings of seventeenth- and eighteenth-century England instilled in him a pervasive skepticism of government officials who often sought to expand their authority at the expense of the rights of their constituents. During his darkest political hour, Jefferson suggested that

> It would be a dangerous delusion were a confidence in the men of our choice to silence our fears for the safety of our rights: that confidence is everywhere the parent of despotism—free government is founded in jealousy, and not in confidence; it is jealousy and not confidence which prescribes limited constitutions, to bind down those whom we are obliged to trust with power. . . .

In questions of power, then, let no more be heard of confidence in man, but bind him down from mischief by the chains of the Constitution.[1]

Jefferson acknowledged the influence of several individuals in shaping his character and philosophy of life. His mother, he readily admitted, had little influence; but his father, who died when Jefferson was only fourteen, was a primary influence. At the age of five, Jefferson attended the English School and four years later the Latin School, where he continued until his father's death. For the next two years Jefferson studied with Anglican minister, James Maury, concentrating on Latin and Greek, literature and mathematics, and the Bible. Although well-trained in the Bible and, like his father, a parish vestryman, Jefferson never accepted the Bible as divine scripture. He read it more as history and readily embraced the philosophical teachings of Jesus.

At the age of seventeen, Jefferson left Shadwell, the family plantation, and attended the College of William and Mary in Williamsburg, Virginia's provincial capital. For the next three years, the lanky, ruddy, freckle-faced youth with tousled reddish-hair, blue-gray eyes, and a sometimes disheveled appearance, studied with Dr. William Small, the college's professor of mathematics, an immigrant from Scotland,

In 1762, Small introduced Jefferson to George Wythe, who at thirty-five, independently wealthy, and self-educated, was becoming the most prominent lawyer in the colony. Wythe not only instructed Jefferson in the law, but introduced him to Governor Francis Fauquier, perhaps the ablest and most popular of Virginia's colonial governors. Forming a *partie quarrée* (a pleasurable party of two couples), Small, Wythe, Jefferson, and the governor regularly dined at the governor's table and conversed on a vari-

1. The Kentucky Resolutions, October 1798, Merrill D. Peterson, ed., *Thomas Jefferson: Writings* (New York, 1984), 454, 455.

ety of topics. Jefferson wrote of these dinners that he "heard more good sense, more rational and philosophical conversations, than in all my life besides." Fauquier also encouraged Jefferson to play his violin at the concerts he sponsored weekly.

When Small returned to Europe in 1762, Jefferson left William and Mary and returned to Shadwell, where he continued reading law under the direction of Wythe, whom Jefferson considered not only his mentor but his foster father. Jefferson expanded his reading and avidly acquired books for his growing library. He was admitted to the bar in 1767, established a successful and growing practice, doubled his estate to 5,000 acres, and decided to design and build a new house. (He saw Shadwell as his mother's house.) Situated across the Rivanna River on the summit of a mountain with a commanding view of the Blue Ridge Mountains to the west and overlooking the valley village of Charlottesville, Jefferson called his new home "Monticello," Italian for "little mountain."

In 1770 disaster struck when Shadwell burned to the ground, and with it, Jefferson's library of almost 700 books worth several hundred pounds. Jefferson wished it had been the money that had gone up in flames; that would have cost him not "a sigh." Immediately, however, Jefferson started rebuilding his literary treasure, and within three years he had a library of 1,256 volumes.

Although Monticello was far from completed when Shadwell burned down, it was advanced enough to convince Jefferson to abandon "some treasonable thoughts of leaving these my native hills."[2] In November 1770, Jefferson moved into a tiny brick cottage at Monticello. "I have here but one room, which, like the cobbler's, serves me for parlor, for kitchen and hall. I may add, for bed chamber and study too." Watching the painfully slow progress on the mansion house, Jefferson could only

2. To John Page, Charlottesville, February 21, 1770, Julian P. Boyd et al., eds., *The Papers of Thomas Jefferson* (Princeton, 1950–), I, 35.

anticipate "getting more elbow room this summer."[3]

But summer passed and Jefferson remained in the cottage. Much of the year, however, Jefferson spent in Williamsburg, where the young lawyer tried cases in the General Court and courted Martha Wayles Skelton, a twenty-three-year-old widow who lived on her father's plantation near Williamsburg. The slender, auburn-haired beauty had been much courted, but she found herself most attracted to the gangly young frontier lawyer. The couple married on January 1, 1772, and journeyed the 100 miles west to spend their first winter together in the cozy "honeymoon" cottage on the mountain. In September 1772 their first child, Martha (usually called Patsy), was born. In May 1773 Jefferson's father-in-law died, leaving his daughter about 5,000 acres and fifty slaves, but also an enormous debt that plagued Jefferson for years.

THE REVOLUTION

In 1769, at the age of twenty-six, Jefferson was elected to the colonial legislature. He proposed but failed to get a bill passed to make it easier for owners to emancipate their slaves. Allied with other young, radical legislators, Jefferson opposed Britain's new imperial policy that attempted to wield greater control over the colonies. The burgesses called for the appointment of committees of correspondence in all of the colonies to coordinate sentiment and activities, and they also called for the appointment of delegates to attend a Continental Congress. Jefferson prepared a petition to the king for Virginia's delegates to Congress, but on the way to take his seat, he was taken ill with dysentery and was unable to attend. He sent copies of his draft petition forward, but the burgesses rejected Jefferson's draft as too radical. Most Americans who opposed British policies argued that Parliament could tax Americans if the tax was primarily aimed at reg-

3. To James Ogilvie, Monticello, February 20, 1771, ibid., I, 63.

ulating commerce. These "external taxes" were constitutional, but "internal taxes" aimed primarily at raising revenue were blatantly unconstitutional. Jefferson went much further, maintaining that Great Britain and the American colonies were totally separate from each other except in loyalty to the same king. Parliament, therefore, had no authority whatsoever to legislate for the colonies, totally opposite of Parliament's Declaratory Act (1766), which asserted Parliament's authority "to bind Americans in all cases whatsoever."

According to Jefferson, his arguments were "read generally by the members, approved by many, but thought too bold for the present state of things."[4] Several friends, however, arranged to have Jefferson's petition printed as a pamphlet under the title *A Summary View of the Rights of British America*. The pamphlet was distributed broadly in America and in Britain, and, according to Jefferson, "procured me the honor of having my name inserted in a long list" of traitors in a bill of attainder that guaranteed his execution.

Jefferson's *Summary View* argued that "History has informed us that bodies of men, as well as individuals, are susceptible of the spirit of tyranny." Parliament and the king's ministers had crossed the line. Since 1763 they had passed a series of acts that threatened American liberty and property. Jefferson declared these acts void, because "the British parliament has no right to exercise authority over us."[5] Under previous British rulers, American rights had been endangered only sporadically. Now, however, a rapid succession of dangerous measures had emanated from London.

> Scarcely have our minds been able to emerge from the astonishment into which one stroke of parliamentary thunder has involved us, before

4. Autobiography (1821), *Jefferson: Writings*, 10.
5. Compare with Jefferson's Kentucky Resolutions of 1798 (below).

another more heavy, and more alarming, is fallen on us. Single acts of tyranny may be ascribed to the accidental opinion of a day; but a series of oppressions, begun at a distinguished period, and pursued unalterably through every change of ministers, too plainly prove a deliberate and systematical plan of reducing us to slavery.

Jefferson urged King George to mediate with Parliament "to recommend . . . the total revocation of these acts, which, however nugatory they be, may yet prove the cause of further discontents and jealousies among us." Americans, like any free people, claim "their rights, as deserved from the laws of nature, and not as the gift of their chief magistrate. Let those flatter who fear: it is not an American art." Jefferson told George III "that kings are the servants, not the proprietors of the people. Open your breast, sire, to liberal and expanded thought. Let not the name of George the third be a blot in the pages of history." America, Jefferson stated, did not wish to separate from Britain. But Jefferson warned the king, "There are extraordinary situations which require extraordinary interposition. An exasperated people, who feel that they possess power, are not easily restrained within limits strictly regular." Jefferson concluded:

The God who gave us life gave us liberty at the same time; the hand of force may destroy, but cannot disjoin them. This, sire, is our last, our determined resolution; and that you will be pleased to interpose with that efficacy which your earnest endeavours may ensure to procure redress of these our great grievances, to quiet the minds of your subjects in British America, against any apprehensions of future encroachment, to establish fraternal love and harmony throughout the whole empire, and that these may continue to the latest ages of time, is the fervent prayer of all British America!

In March 1775 the Virginia provincial convention added Jefferson to its delegation to the Second Continental Congress. Before Congress assembled, the first shots of the Revolution were fired at Lexington and Concord, Massachusetts. Congress drafted petitions to Britain seeking reconciliation and justifying why Americans had taken up arms. Jefferson prepared a draft declaration explaining America's position, but it was too strong for many of the delegates. John Dickinson of Delaware wrote the Declaration of the Causes and Necessity of Taking up Arms in July 1775. Unable to improve upon Jefferson's closing four paragraphs, Dickinson incorporated them into his draft, which Congress accepted. The rhetoric of these paragraphs was characteristically Jefferson's—powerful, eloquent, stirring. It surely angered the king and probably made reconciliation impossible.

The force and beauty of Jefferson's closing paragraphs still have remarkable impact: "We are reduced to the alternative of choosing an unconditional submission to the tyranny of irritated ministers, or resistance by force. The latter is our choice. . . . Honor, justice, and humanity forbid us tamely to surrender that freedom which we received from our gallant ancestors, and which our innocent posterity have a right to receive from us."

"Our cause is just. Our union is perfect. Our internal resources are great, and, if necessary, foreign assistance is undoubtedly attainable." He thanked God for not permitting the crisis of British domination to occur "until we were grown up to our present strength" and had gained needed experience fighting a previous war.

Americans, Jefferson wrote, did not seek independence from Britain. "Necessity has not yet driven us into that desperate measure, or induced us to excite any other

nation to war against" Britain. But Americans were determined to protect their rights and their property with an
"unabating firmness and perseverance, . . . being with one
mind resolved to die freemen rather than to live slaves."

American petitions, resolutions, and declarations
never swayed Parliament, the ministry, or King George.
Quite the contrary. King and Parliament declared the
colonists in a state of rebellion. Abandoning efforts at reconciliation, the British attacked with overwhelming military power in an attempt to intimidate Americans into
submission. Most Americans, too, became convinced that
reconciliation was impossible. The necessity for independence absent in July 1775 appeared full blown a year
later, but not all of the delegates in Congress were in
agreement when Virginia moved on June 7, 1776, that the
"United Colonies are, and of right ought to be, free and
independent states." It was decided, therefore, to post-
pone a vote on independence for almost four weeks.
Congress appointed committees to seek foreign assistance
and alliances, to draft articles of union, and to draft a
declaration of independence. The declaration committee consisted of John Adams, Benjamin Franklin, Robert
R. Livingston, Roger Sherman, and Thomas Jefferson.
The committee chose the thirty-three-year-old Virginian
to draft the Declaration.

It is unclear how the committee selected Jefferson to
draft the Declaration, how he wrote it, and how it was
eventually presented to Congress. A quarter century later
Adams remembered that

> Mr. Jefferson had been now about a Year a
> Member of Congress, but had attended his Duty
> in the House but a very small part of the time and
> when there had never spoken in public: and during
> the whole Time I sat with him in Congress, I never
> heard him utter three Sentences together . . .
> It will naturally be inquired, how it happened that

he was appointed on a Committee of such importance. There were more reasons than one. Mr. Jefferson had the Reputation of a masterly Pen. He had been chosen a Delegate in Virginia, in consequence of a very handsome public Paper, which he had written for the House of Burgesses, which had given him the Character of a fine Writer. Another reason was that Mr. Richard Henry Lee was not beloved by the most of his Colleagues from Virginia and Mr. Jefferson was set up to rival and supplant him. This could be done only by the Pen, for Mr. Jefferson could stand no competition with him or any one else in Elocution and public debate. . . . The Committee had several meetings, in which were proposed the Articles of which the Declaration was to consist, and minutes made of them. The Committee then appointed Mr. Jefferson and me, to draw them up in form, and cloath them in a proper Dress. The Sub Committee met, and considered the Minutes, making such Observations on them as then occurred; when Mr. Jefferson desired me to take them to my Lodgings and make the Draft. This I declined and gave several reasons for declining. 1. That he was a Virginian and I a Massachusettsian. 2. that he was a southern Man and I a northern one. 3. That I had been so obnoxious for my early and constant Zeal in promoting the Measure, that any draft of mine, would undergo a more severe Scrutiny and Criticism in Congress, than one of his composition. 4thly and lastly and that would be reason enough if there were no other, I had a great Opinion of the Elegance of his pen and none at all of my own. I therefore insisted that no hesitation should be made on his part. He accordingly took the Minutes and in a day or two produced to me his Draft. Whether I made or suggested any corrections I remember not. The Report was made to the Committee of five, by them examined, but whether altered or corrected in any thing I cannot recollect. But in substance at least it was reported to Congress where, after a severe Criticism, and striking out several of the most oratorical Paragraphs it was adopted on the fourth of July 1776, and published to the World.[6]

Jefferson wrote the Declaration of Independence in the seclusion of his parlor in his small second-floor apartment in a new three-story brick building on Market Street between Seventh and Eighth streets in Philadelphia. One can only imagine what his thoughts were as he stared down at a blank sheet of paper upon his new "writing-box." Charged with writing a document to justify America's attempt to become an independent nation, the Declaration should inspire the American people and obtain support from abroad—within Britain as well as among Britain's enemies. In another sense, Jefferson wanted to address a much broader audience—all of posterity—both those who would seek to live their lives in liberty as well as those who would seek to dominate over others. Years later, only about a year before his death, Jefferson explained what the Declaration of Independence was supposed to do.

When forced, therefore, to resort to arms for redress, an appeal to the tribunal of the world was deemed proper for our justification. This was the object of the Declaration of Independence. Not to find out new principles, or new arguments, never before thought of, not merely to say things

6. John Adams Autobiography (1802), L. H. Butterfield et al., eds., *Diary and Autobiography of John Adams* (4 vols., Cambridge, Mass., 1962), III, 335–37.

which had never been said before; but to place before mankind the common sense of the subject, in terms so plain and firm as to command their assent, and to justify ourselves in the independent stand we are compelled to take. Neither aiming at originality of principle or sentiment, nor yet copied from any particular and previous writing, it was intended to be an expression of the American mind, and to give to that expression the proper tone and spirit called for by the occasion. All its authority rests then on the harmonizing sentiments of the day, whether expressed in conversation, in letters, printed essays, or in the elementary books of public right, as Aristotle, Cicero, Locke, Sidney, &c.[7]

The genius of Thomas Jefferson is that he infused the Declaration with "the proper tone and spirit called for." Jefferson took a huge body of political literature—22,000 pamphlets published in Britain in the seventeenth century and several thousand more published during the eighteenth in Britain and America—and condensed it into five sentences, a total of 202 words: the introduction to the Declaration of Independence. These five sentences constitute arguably what is the greatest statement in political literature.

We hold these truths to be self-evident, that all men are created equal, that they are endowed by their Creator with certain unalienable Rights, that among these are Life, Liberty and the pursuit of Happiness,—That to secure these rights, Governments are instituted among Men, deriving their just powers from the consent of the governed,—That whenever any Form of Government becomes destructive of these ends, it

7. To Henry Lee, Monticello, May 8, 1825, *Jefferson: Writings*, 1501.

is the Right of the People to alter or to abolish it; and to institute new Government, laying its foundation on such principles and organizing its powers in such form, as to them shall seem most likely to effect their Safety and Happiness. Prudence, indeed, will dictate that Governments long established should not be changed for light and transient causes; and accordingly all experience hath shewn, that mankind are more disposed to suffer, while evils are sufferable. But when a long train of abuses and usurpations, pursuing invariably the same Object evinces a design to reduce them under absolute Despotism, it is their right, it is their duty, to throw off such Government, and to provide new Guards for their future security.

Jefferson's truth may be self-evident, but "the pursuit of Happiness" has baffled many. The simplest explanation is that this phrase is a euphemistic synonym for "property," similar to John Locke's "life, liberty, and estate." Jefferson, however, meant far more than the right to buy, possess, and dispose of property. He wanted a government that, in the words of John Adams, "communicates ease, comfort, [and] security"[8]—a government that would provide protection from foreign invasion, from assault by criminals (and attack by Indians in America), and from oppressive government rule and taxation. Government, according to Jefferson, should provide an efficient, well-run economic environment as well as a society where contrary religious and political opinions could exist in harmony—where the majority ruled but with due deference to the rights of the minority. After playing its role in leveling the field, government would step aside and interfere no more. In his first inaugural address as president in March 1801, Jefferson himself explained the role of government in the pursuit of happiness: "A wise and frugal

8. Adams, *Thoughts on Government . . . 1776, Adams Papers*, IV, 86.

Government, which shall restrain men from injuring one another, shall leave them otherwise free to regulate their own pursuits of industry and improvement, and shall not take from the mouth of labor the bread it has earned. This is the sum of good government, and this is necessary to close the circle of our felicities."[9]

THE REFORMER

While Jefferson was attending Congress in Philadelphia his mind was on events in Williamsburg where delegates in a provincial convention were drafting and adopting a bill of rights and a new state constitution for Virginia. (In fact, the Declaration of Rights, adopted on June 12, 1776, probably informed Jefferson's Declaration of Independence.) Three hundred miles away from home, Jefferson drafted his own constitution and sent it to George Wythe. Jefferson's constitution retained the structure of Virginia's colonial government but provided nearly universal adult male suffrage. He wanted both houses of the legislature and the governor elected annually, with the governor, stripped of his veto power, ineligible for reelection for five years. Except for the wording of the constitution's preamble, the convention ignored Jefferson's proposal in favor of a constitution that favored the wealthy Tidewater planters. For the rest of his life Jefferson chafed at Virginia's constitution, but he never realized any meaningful change.

When the first Virginia House of Delegates assembled in October 1776, Jefferson attended. Using the principles espoused in the Declaration of Independence, Jefferson hoped to rid Virginia of the last vestiges of feudalism and aristocratic favoritism. In mid-October 1776 Jefferson suggested that the House appoint a committee

9. For more on Jefferson's description of good government that would contribute to the happiness of the people, see the discussion of Jefferson's first inaugural address below.

to revise the state's laws. Two weeks later the House appointed a committee of five, chaired by Jefferson, that included George Wythe. It took the committee three years to submit its final report—a thorough reformation of the law on republican and liberal principles—by which time Jefferson, no longer in the House, was unable to shepherd the new laws into being.

The legislature considered some reforms immediately. Jefferson, ever the advocate of republicanism and the widespread ownership of property, successfully campaigned for the abolition of entail, the feudal relic that required inherited property to pass intact to heirs. Later primogeniture (the inheritance of estates by the eldest son) and the system of quitrents (a lifetime rental system) were disallowed, thus guaranteeing a broader ownership of land.

Jefferson's reforms sought to moderate Virginia's harsh criminal code. He proposed reducing the numerous capital offenses to two—murder and treason—and rejected corporal punishment as well as the newfangled policy of long-term imprisonment. Instead, Jefferson favored a broad system of public service for criminals, who would wear uniforms and whose heads would be shaved to prevent escape. In the mid–1780s, when Jefferson was in Europe, James Madison supported these modifications in the criminal code, but with little success. It would take another ten years before Jefferson's ideas would be adopted.

Jefferson also supported the complete separation of church and state. Although the Virginia Declaration of Rights provided that "all men are equally entitled to the free exercise of religion, according to the dictates of conscience," and the state constitution discontinued the official establishment of the Anglican Church, Jefferson felt that a more explicit separation of church and state was needed. In 1779 he drafted a Bill for Religious Freedom. Like most of his reforms, it lay dormant. In 1783, Patrick Henry, Edmund Pendleton, and Richard Henry Lee proposed public support for Christian Protestant ministers. James Madison now revived and championed Jefferson's bill in the House of Delegates, and in January 1786 the bill was adopted. It provided:

> that the opinions of men are not the object of civil government, nor under its jurisdiction. . . . that no man shall be compelled to frequent or support any religious worship, place, or ministry whatsoever, nor shall be enforced, restrained, molested, or burdened in his body or goods, nor shall otherwise suffer, on account of his religious opinions or belief; but that all men shall be free to profess, and by argument to maintain, their opinions in matters of religion, and that the same shall in no wise diminish, enlarge, or affect their civil capacities.

Jefferson was most proud of this act. He also greatly admired the way in which religious freedom was protected in the First Amendment of the U.S. Constitution. In an address to the Baptist Association of Danbury, Connecticut, on January 1, 1802, President Jefferson reiterated his support for "a wall of separation between Church & State."[10]

Jefferson was also a staunch advocate for reform in public education. He submitted a Bill for the More General Diffusion of Knowledge in 1779, which called for a three-tiered system of public education—elementary, general, and university. All free children would be educated for three years at public expense. The best students—the state's "natural aristocracy" of merit and virtue—would advance from one level to the next with public support. Other children could continue their education, but without public support. Jefferson told Wythe that "by far the most important bill in our whole code is that for the diffusion of knowledge among the people. No other sure foundation can be devised, for the preservation

10. *Jefferson: Writings*, 510.

of freedom and happiness."[11] Neither Jefferson nor Wythe could get the educational reforms adopted. Support for comprehensive public education in Virginia would have to wait until after the Civil War.

In May 1779 the Virginia legislature elected Jefferson governor. He did not want the job but believed that "In a virtuous government, and more especially in times like these, public offices are, what they should be, burdens to those appointed to them which it would be wrong to decline, though foreseen to bring with them intense labor and great private loss."[12] It was the worst time to be governor of a Southern state. The British had abandoned their strategy of separating New England from New York and had transferred their military initiatives to the South, capturing Savannah in December 1778 and Charleston in May 1780. Several amphibious assaults against Virginia took place during this time and the British army, commanded by General Charles Cornwallis, relentlessly marched northward toward Virginia. On May 20 Cornwallis captured Richmond, Virginia's new capital, forcing the Patriot government to evacuate to Charlottesville. Cornwallis sent a detachment of rangers to capture the government. Warned just in time, government officials hastily fled across the Blue Ridge Mountains to Staunton. At Monticello, Jefferson was also warned and escaped to a nearby mountaintop where he watched the British in Charlottesville through his telescope. The British left Monticello undamaged but wreaked destruction on other property, including Jefferson's farm at Elk Hill.

Although Jefferson's term as governor had expired on June 2, he was blamed by those who looked for a scapegoat for the British devastation because there was no adequate defense. Former governor Patrick Henry, who had led the opposition to Jefferson's reform program, called for an investigation. Finding no evidence of either wrong-

11. To George Wythe, Paris, August 13, 1786, *Jefferson: Writings*, 859.
12. Quoted in Norman K. Risjord, *Thomas Jefferson* (Madison, Wis., 1994), 42.

doing or cowardice, the House of Delegates passed a resolution affirming "the high opinion which they entertain of Mr. Jefferson's Ability, Rectitude, and Integrity as chief Magistrate of this Commonwealth, and mean by thus publicly avowing their opinion, to obviate and remove all unmerited Censure."[13] The charges against him, however, had done severe damage to Jefferson's reputation and to his attitude about public service. Jefferson vowed never to serve in public office again.

JEFFERSON AND SLAVERY

Throughout his life Jefferson wrestled with the problem of slavery.[14] He, like most Americans, denounced the foreign slave trade that captured free men, women, and children in Africa, forcibly transported them in the most inhumane fashion to the Western Hemisphere, and sold them as property into lifelong bondage. As a first-year legislator in 1769, and in drafting the Declaration of Independence seven years later, Jefferson had denounced the foreign slave trade. Not until 1782, when Jefferson was temporarily retired from public service, did Virginia prohibit the foreign slave trade. Then, as president in December 1806, Jefferson proposed to Congress that the foreign slave trade be prohibited as of January 1, 1808 (the earliest allowable date for a congressional prohibition under the Constitution). Congress enacted the bill on March 2, 1807, and President Jefferson signed it the next day.

Jefferson also consistently denounced the institution of slavery in principle. His attitude toward emancipation and toward blacks was more complex. In 1781, as the Revolution neared its conclusion, Jefferson denounced the incongruity of fighting a revolution for liberty while keeping a race of people in bondage. "Indeed," Jefferson

13. Quoted in Risjord, *Thomas Jefferson,* 47.

14. For more on Jefferson's attitude toward slavery, see John P. Kaminski, ed., *A Necessary Evil?: Slavery and the Debate Over the Constitution* (Madison, Wis., 1995).

wrote, "I tremble for my country when I reflect that God is just: that his justice cannot sleep for ever." Jefferson deplored not only the injustice done to blacks, but the unhealthy effect—political, social, moral, and economic—that slavery had on whites. "There must doubtless be an unhappy influence on the manners of our people produced by the existence of slavery among us. The whole commerce between master and slave is a perpetual exercise of the most boisterous passions, the most unremitting despotism on the one part, and degrading submissions on the other."[15]

In the mid–1780s Jefferson saw the institution of slavery as a conflict between "justice" and "avarice & oppression." He looked to the youth of revolutionary America who "have sucked in the principles of liberty as it were with their mother's milk" to abolish the evil institution.[16] After his presidency, Jefferson continued to denounce slavery.

> The love of justice and the love of country plead equally the cause of these people, and it is a mortal reproach to us that they should have pleaded it so long in vain, and should have produced not a single effort, nay I fear not much serious willingness to relieve them & ourselves from our present condition of moral & political reprobation.[17]

When asked to participate in several plans for emancipation, Jefferson reiterated his eagerness to end slavery. "There is nothing," he wrote, "I would not sacrifice to a practicable plan of abolishing every vestige of this moral and political depravity."[18] But Jefferson also saw many obstacles to emancipation. Metaphorically he described slavery as having "the wolf by the ear, and we can neither

15. *Notes on the State of Virginia*, 1782, *Jefferson: Writings*, 289, 288.

16. To Richard Price, Paris, August 7, 1785, *Jefferson Papers*, VIII, 357.

17. To Edward Coles, Monticello, August 25, 1814, *Jefferson: Writings*, 1344, 1346.

18. To Thomas Cooper, Monticello, September 10, 1814, *A Necessary Evil*, 263.

hold him, nor safely let him go." Now, instead of justice versus avarice and oppression, Jefferson saw the dilemma as "Justice is in one scale, and self-preservation in the other."[19] And he refused either to be an active participant or even a silent, behind-the-scenes supporter of emancipation. That was for a future generation.

Jefferson hoped for emancipation, but he saw it happening only if three parts of a coordinated plan could be implemented: (1) gradual and compensated emancipation in which slaveowners would be paid from public funds for their financial loss; (2) colonization of free blacks, preferably to Africa, but more likely to some Caribbean island nation; and (3) replacement of the black labor force with a free alternative—most likely Protestant Germans similar to those who had immigrated to Pennsylvania. Jefferson felt that colonization was required because of racism. He had come to the conclusion that blacks were inferior to whites and thus the intermingling of blood should be avoided at all costs. Furthermore blacks would forever hate whites for the evils perpetrated against them. Conflict was thus inevitable if the two races lived close together. But because the practicalities of such a plan prohibited it from being implemented when most slaves remained in the South, Jefferson came to advocate the diffusion of slavery throughout America, especially to the West. Only in this way could a similar nationwide attitude and appreciation for the problem be realized. Until his death, Jefferson hoped that this terrible problem could be solved. "The abolition of the evil is not impossible; it ought never therefore to be despaired of. Every plan should be adopted, every experiment tried, which may do something towards the ultimate object."[20] But Jefferson himself would not participate in any such plan.

19. To John Holmes, Monticello, April 22, 1820, *Jefferson: Writings*, 1434.

20. To Frances Wright, Monticello, August 7, 1825, H. A. Washington, ed., *The Writings of Thomas Jefferson* (9 vols., Washington, D.C., 1853–1854), VII, 408.

AT HOME

Jefferson returned to Monticello in September 1781 "to my farm, my family and books from which I think nothing will evermore separate me."[21] Immediately visitors started descending on Monticello. Major General the Marquis de Chastellux described the former governor after a four-day visit.

> Let me describe to you a man, not yet forty, tall, and with a mild and pleasing countenance, but whose mind and understanding are ample substitutes for every exterior grace. An American, who without ever having quitted his own country, is at once a musician, skilled in drawing; a geometrician, an astronomer, a natural philosopher, legislator, and statesman. A senator of America, who sat for two years in that famous Congress which brought about the revolution; and which is never mentioned without respect, though unhappily not without *regret*; a governor of Virginia, who filled this difficult station during the invasions of Arnold, of Philips, and of Cornwallis; a philosopher, in voluntary retirement, from the world, and public business, because he loves them, inasmuch only as he can flatter himself with being useful to mankind; and the minds of his countrymen are not yet in a condition either to bear the light, or to suffer contradiction. A mild and amiable wife, charming children, of whose education he himself takes charge, a house to embellish, great provisions to improve, and the arts and sciences to cultivate; these are what remain to Mr. Jefferson, after having played a principal character on the theater of the new world, and which he preferred to the honorable commission of Minister Plenipotentiary in Europe. The visit

21. To Edmund Randolph, Monticello, September 16, 1781, *Jefferson Papers*, VI, 118.

which I made him was not unexpected, for he had long since invited me to come and pass a few days with him, in the center of the mountains; notwithstanding which I found his first appearance serious, nay even cold; but before I had been two hours with him we were as intimate as if we had passed our whole lives together; walking, books, but above all, a conversation always varied and interesting, always supported by that sweet satisfaction experienced by two persons, who in communicating their sentiments and opinions, are invariably in unison, and who understand each other at the first hint, made four days pass away like so many minutes.[22]

On May 8, 1782, Martha Jefferson gave birth to their sixth child, Lucy Elizabeth (three of their six children had previously died in infancy). Martha Jefferson never recovered from the childbirth. Perhaps anemia sapped her strength as she steadily weakened before Jefferson's eyes. For four months she languished as Jefferson watched over her almost constantly. For almost three months he did not write a letter. Finally, on September 6, she died. Jefferson collapsed in her bedroom. A period of deep mourning followed. He destroyed his entire correspondence with Martha. His three daughters were sent away, and friends feared that Jefferson too might die. For weeks he incessantly paced in his library, then started riding around his farms on horseback for hours at a time. A concerned James Madison saw that "Perhaps this domestic catastrophe may prove in its operation beneficial to his country by weaning him from those attachments which deprived it of his services."[23] Madison convinced Congress to add Jefferson to

22. Marquis de Chastellux: *Travels in North-America, in the Years 1780, 1781, and 1782* (2 vols., London, 1787).

23. Madison to Edmund Randolph, September 30, 1782, William T. Hutchinson et al., eds., *The Papers of James Madison* (Chicago and Charlottesville, 1962–), V, 120.

the ongoing peace negotiations in Paris. Jefferson, who had always wanted to visit Europe, leaped at the chance to leave Monticello. He went to Baltimore to await transport on a French warship, but before they departed word arrived that a preliminary peace treaty had been signed, and Congress rescinded his appointment. Jefferson went back to Monticello and worked on a revision of the Virginia constitution, catalogued his library of 2,640 books, and supervised the education of his two older daughters and a nephew.

CONGRESSIONAL LEADER

In June 1783, the Virginia legislature appointed Jefferson a delegate to Congress beginning in November. Jefferson decided to bring Patsy, his eldest daughter, with him to Philadelphia so that she could acquire "a little taste and execution in such of the fine arts as she could not prosecute to equal advantage in a more retired situation."[24] They arrived in Philadelphia in early November only to find that Congress intended to move to Annapolis. Jefferson arranged for Patsy's accommodations and "procure[d] for her the best tutors in French, dancing, music & drawing."[25] Jefferson left Philadelphia on November 22; three days later he arrived in Annapolis eager to begin the work of a new country.

Immediately Jefferson became a leader in Congress. In acknowledgment of his literary skills, Jefferson was chosen to write Congress' response to George Washington when the commander-in-chief surrendered his commission on December 23, 1783. During Congress' five-month session, Jefferson wrote reports for at least thirty-one committees. One report proposed a radical new national system of coinage, abandoning the familiar English system in favor of a decimal system based upon the dollar. Not immediate-

24. Jefferson to the Marquis de Barbé–Marbois, Annapolis, December 5, 1783, Paul H. Smith, ed., *Letters of Delegates to Congress, 1774–1789* (26 vols., Washington, D.C., 1976–2000), XXI, 182.

25. Jefferson to James Monroe, Philadelphia, November 18, 1783, ibid., 156.

ly adopted, the report served as the model for the system that was eventually adopted in 1794.

In 1781 Governor Jefferson was instrumental in getting Virginia to cede its huge territory north and west of the Ohio River to Congress. Such a cession benefited Congress, placated other states (especially those with no western lands), and, under the prevailing theory of Baron de Montesquieu that republics could not survive in large territories, would help assure the liberties of Virginians. Now in Congress, Jefferson drafted the Land Ordinance of 1784 that provided for the administration of the Northwest Territory and the admittance of new states into the union on an equal basis with the original thirteen states. Unfortunately, by the vote of a single delegate, Congress removed Jefferson's prohibition of slavery and indentured servitude from the Northwest Territory. (Such prohibitions would be reestablished in the Northwest Ordinance of 1787.)

Jefferson also had an interest in the western lands beyond the borders of the United States. According to the recently adopted Treaty of Peace, the Mississippi River served as America's western border. Although Spain claimed the territory west of the Mississippi, information had been received that "a very large sum of money" had been raised in England to explore the land between the Mississippi and the Pacific Ocean. Ostensibly the proposed expedition had only scientific goals, but Jefferson feared that the British "have thoughts of colonizing into that quarter." Jefferson and others began raising funds for an American expedition of discovery. Although he feared that Americans did not possess "enough of that kind of spirit to raise the money," he sounded out fellow-Virginian George Rogers Clark, the Revolutionary War hero of battles in Illinois and Indiana, to see if he would be willing "to lead such a party."[26] Jefferson's interest in the West never waned. Twenty years would pass before

26. Jefferson to Clark, Annapolis, December 4, 1783, *Jefferson: Writings*, 783.

President Jefferson purchased this expansive territory thus doubling the size of the United States. He then chose Meriwether Lewis and William Clark (George Rogers Clark's brother) to lead an expedition to the Pacific.

While in Annapolis, Jefferson took an active role in directing the education of his daughter in Philadelphia and Peter Carr, his nephew, in Virginia. As always, Jefferson believed that education had academic, vocational, physical, and moral components. To Peter, he sent a copy of Homer along with the admonition to obey his teacher and not to waste time. "You are now old enough to know how very important to your future life will be the manner in which you employ your present time. I hope therefore you will never waste a moment of it."[27] Jefferson would repeat this advice continually to youth studying under his direction. "Consider how little time is left you, and how much you have to attain in it, and that every moment you lose of it is lost for ever." "Time is now the most pressing and precious thing in the world to you, and the greatest injury which can possibly be done you is to waste what remains."[28]

To Patsy, he outlined her daily schedule: wake up at sunrise and breakfast, from 8:00 to 10:00 practice music, from 10:00 to 1:00 dance one day and draw another, from 1:00 to 2:00 draw on the day you dance and write a letter the next day, from 2 to 3:00 dine, from 3 to 4:00 read French, from 4 to 5:00 exercise to music, and from 5:00 till bedtime read English and write.[29] In writing, Jefferson told his daughter "Take care that you never spell a word wrong." If uncertain of the spelling, "turn to a dictionary." It was important to present a proper image in correspondence as well as in person. He told Patsy to keep his letters and refer to them "that you may always have present in your mind those things which will endear you to me."

27. Annapolis, December 11, 1783, *Jefferson Papers*, VI, 379.
28. To Francis Eppes, Monticello, October 6, 1820, and, Poplar Forest, December 13, 1820, Jefferson Papers, Library of Congress.
29. Annapolis, November 28, 1783, *Jefferson: Writings*, 782.

Jefferson advised Patsy to be wary of religious zealots in Philadelphia who predicted the imminent destruction of the earth.[30]

> The almighty has never made known to any body at what time he created it, nor will he tell any body when he means to put an end to it, if ever he means to do it. As to preparations for that event, the best way is for you to be always prepared for it. . . . never to do nor say a bad thing. If ever you are about to say any thing amiss or to do any thing wrong, consider before hand. You will feel something within you which will tell you it is wrong and ought not to be said or done: this is your conscience, and be sure to obey it. Our maker has given us all, this faithful internal Monitor, and if you always obey it, you will always be prepared for the end of the world: or for a much more certain event which is death. This must happen to all: it puts an end to the world as to us, and the way to be ready for it is never to do a wrong act.[31]

SERVICE ABROAD

After the war for independence, Congress wanted to establish diplomatic and commercial relations with all countries. Congress appointed a three-man commission to negotiate commercial treaties with European and North African countries. Benjamin Franklin and John Adams, both still in France, were obvious appointments. Needing a southerner to round out the commission, Congress appointed Jefferson on May 7, 1784. Without going home, Jefferson wrote letters to friends and family to provide for the supervision of his plantation and the safekeeping of his two daughters in Virginia. On May 11 Jefferson left Annapolis for Philadelphia. Taking Patsy with him, they traveled through New England where

30. Ibid., 783.
31. Annapolis, December 11, 1783, ibid., 784.

Jefferson learned as much as he could about commercial matters. On July 5 the Jeffersons set sail from Boston on the merchant ship *Ceres*. Despite all the horror stories told about Atlantic crossings, their nineteen-day voyage was uneventful. Patsy likened it to floating down a river. Not so the harrowing thirteen-hour crossing of the tempestuous English Channel.

Arrived in Paris in August 1784, both father and daughter shed their provincial attire and purchased new wardrobes fashionable for Paris. Patsy, enrolled in an exclusive Catholic convent school in which religion was excluded from the curriculum, adjusted easily, but her father struggled. His lack of conversational French hampered his ability to communicate, and the dampness of the weather and unwholesomeness of the water caused him considerable suffering during the "seasoning" process.[32] In January 1785 Jefferson's anguish heightened when he learned of the death of two-year-old Lucy. The awful news sent Jefferson into a deep depression for several months. With the warmth of spring, Jefferson felt well enough to resume his duties. He wrote his brother-in-law to ask that Polly be sent to Europe as soon as practicable. (It would take over two years before Polly would join her father and sister in Paris.)

In late February 1785 Congress appointed John Adams minister plenipotentiary to Great Britain, and in early May, John and Abigail Adams left France. Abigail hated to leave "Mr. Jefferson, he is one of the choice ones of the Earth,"[33] and "the only person with whom my Companion could associate; with perfect freedom, and unreserve."[34]

In May 1785 Congress approved Benjamin Franklin's request to return to America and unanimously elected Jefferson to replace him as U.S. minister to France.

32. To James Monroe, Paris, March 18, 1785, *Jefferson Papers*, VIII, 43.

33. To Mary Cranch, May 8, 1785, L. H. Butterfield et al., eds., *Adams Family Correspondence* (Cambridge, Mass., 1963–), VI, 119.

34. To Thomas Jefferson, London, June 6, 1785, ibid., VI, 169.

Franklin returned to America in July. Because of the veneration the French had for Franklin, Jefferson knew that the transition could be difficult. He described it "as an excellent school of humility." When presented as the new American minister, the usual question was *"c'est vous, Monsieur, qui remplace le Docteur Franklin?"* Jefferson generally answered, "no one can replace him, Sir: I am only his successor."[35]

Jefferson worked tirelessly to improve commercial relations with France, its Caribbean colonies, and with other countries. Treaties were signed with Prussia and Morocco. The Marquis de Lafayette greatly assisted Jefferson in commercial matters, not only in France, but in Spain as well. According to Jefferson, the young Frenchman's zeal was unbounded. He was "a most valuable auxiliary."[36] Lafayette was equally praising of Jefferson. "No better minister could be sent to France. He is everything that is good, upright, enlightened, and clever, and is respected and beloved by everyone that knows him."[37] To George Washington, Lafayette wrote that "Words cannot sufficiently express to you how much I am pleased with Mr. Jefferson's public conduct—He unites every ability that can recommend him with the ministers, and at the [same] time possesses accomplishments of the mind and the heart which cannot but give him many friends."[38] Lafayette was delighted to be Jefferson's "Aid de Camp."[39] "His abilities, His Virtues, His temper, Every thing of Him Commands Respect and

35. To the Rev. William Smith, Philadelphia, February 19, 1791, *Jefferson: Writings*, 975.

36. To James Madison, Paris, January 30, 1787, *Madison Papers*, IX, 250.

37. Marquis de Lafayette to James McHenry, Paris, December 3, 1785, Stanley J. Idzerda et al., eds., *Lafayette in the Age of the American Revolution: Selected Letters and Papers, 1776–1790* (5 vols., Ithaca, N.Y., 1977–83), V, 355.

38. Paris, February 6, 1786, *Washington Papers*, Conf. Ser., III, 545.

39. To George Washington, Paris, October 26, 1786, ibid., IV, 311.

Attracts Affection. He Enjoys Universal Regard, and does the Affairs of America to perfection. It is the Happiest choice that Could Be Made."[40]

In addition to opening new markets for American exports in both Europe and the Caribbean, Jefferson sent exotic plants back to America—he sent upland rice and beans from Italy to South Carolina, olive trees and shoots to Baltimore, and Spanish merino sheep and grape vines were sent to Washington. The introduction of a new crop to a country was, in Jefferson's opinion, "worth more to them than all the victories of the most splendid pages of their history."[41] To his friends Madison and Monroe, as well as others, he sent books—food for the mind—on a wide variety of subjects. Two decades later, a good friend from the National Gardens in Paris returned the favor when he sent Jefferson over 700 different species of flowers.

At the request of Adams, Jefferson visited England in March and April 1785 to assist in negotiating commercial treaties with the Portuguese minister to England and with a diplomatic agent from Tripoli. While in London, Adams arranged to have Jefferson presented to the king and queen at one of their levees. As Adams and Jefferson approached the monarchs, the king turned his back on them. Jefferson wrote that "it was impossible for anything to be more ungracious." In this instant, Jefferson clearly saw "the ulcerations in the narrow mind of that mulish being."[42] Jefferson felt that free trade and "peace and friendship with all mankind is our wisest policy; . . . but the temper and folly of our enemies may not leave this in our choice."[43]

Difficult negotiations took place between the U.S.

40. Marquis de Lafayette to George Washington, Paris, January 1, 1788, ibid., VI, 6.

41. To Alexandre Giroud, Philadelphia, May 22, 1797, *Jefferson Papers*, XXIX, 387.

42. Autobiography (1821), *Jefferson: Writings*, 57.

43. To C. W. F. Dumas, Paris, May 6, 1786, *Jefferson Papers*, IX, 463.

and the Barbary States of North Africa—Morocco, Algiers, Tripoli, and Tunis. No longer under the protection of the British Navy, American merchant vessels were preyed upon by predatory pirates sanctioned by the governments of these countries. Several American ships had already been seized and their crews and passengers enslaved by the Moroccans and the Algerines. Through the good graces of the Spanish, the Moroccans signed a treaty and released the hostages and the ship *Betsy*. Algiers, however, rejected all American overtures and refused to lessen its exorbitant ransom demands. John Adams advised paying the ransom as the cheapest way to handle the problem; Jefferson favored war as the best means of obtaining a lasting peace. Jefferson proposed a confederation of small countries to oppose the Algerines. He also recommended that Congress create a small navy of 150 guns that would cruise the Mediterranean to protect American merchantmen. Such a policy would promote justice by punishing the aggressor, provide honor and respect (which would safeguard future American interests), and produce the least internal danger to the rights of Americans from an empowered Confederation government. (Jefferson, as well as most Americans of this period, feared that a standing army would endanger liberties.) Furthermore a just war against so weak an opponent was opportune.[44] Congress, however, opposed war, negotiations dragged on, and American hostages remained enslaved for over ten years.

Jefferson enjoyed the architecture, museums, and formal gardens in and around Paris. He so enjoyed French cuisine that he brought one of his slaves, John Hemings, to Paris to be trained as a French chef. He came to have a real affection for France and the French people. He felt that France was "The only nation on earth on whom we

44. To John Adams, Paris, July 11, 1786, *Jefferson Papers*, X, 123; Autobiography (1821), *Jefferson: Writings*, 59–61.

can solidly rely for assistance till we can stand on our own legs."[45] He told Abigail Adams that Frenchmen "have as much happiness in one year as an Englishman in ten."[46] It was "impossible to be among a people who wish more to make one happy, a people of the very best character it is possible for one to have. We have no idea in America of the real French character."[47] It was difficult, he readily admitted, to understand the French. "A Frenchman never says *No*: and it is difficult for a stranger to know when he means it. Perhaps it is the longest to be learnt of all the particularities of the nation."[48] But if you asked the seasoned traveler of any nation, "In what country on earth would you rather live?" They would naturally say their own, but their second choice would always be France.[49]

Jefferson walked four or five miles daily among the tree-lined pathways and fountains of Bois de Boulogne. It was on one of Jefferson's many sightseeing excursions that he spotted John Trumbull, the young Connecticut painter, whom Jefferson had first met a few months earlier in London. Trumbull introduced Jefferson to Richard and Maria Cosway, fellow painters from London. Immediately Jefferson was smitten with Maria's charm and beauty. She too was taken with the tall, handsome diplomat, who, in most ways was the complete opposite of her short, foppish, dissolute husband. When Trumbull left for Germany and Richard Cosway busied himself painting portraits of the French nobility, Jefferson and Maria toured the Parisian countryside by days and half days. Jefferson had now been a widower for four years, and he easily succumbed to the Italian-born beauty. Whether their relationship was consummated or remained merely flirtatious is impossible to know. But Jefferson felt "more dead than alive" when the Cosways left Paris to

45. To Ralph Izard, Paris, November 18, 1786, *Jefferson Papers*, X, 541–42.

46. Paris, August 9, 1786, ibid., 203.

47. To Eliza House Trist, Paris, December 15, 1786, ibid., 600.

48. To Thomas Paine, Paris, July 3, 1788, ibid., XIII, 307.

49. Autobiography (1821), *Jefferson: Writings*, 98.

return to London. Seated by his fireplace "solitary and sad," he wrote one of the great love letters of all time—a dialogue between his head and his heart, where the head warned against such relationships but the heart rejoiced in all the pleasures and pain of life. A devout Catholic, Maria could never divorce. She did, however, on several occasions leave her husband and reside on the Continent. But travel to America was out of the question: she was deathly afraid of ocean travel. And so when Jefferson planned his return to America in 1789, he wrote Maria that "When wafting on the bosom of the ocean I shall pray it to be as calm and smooth as yours to me." The ardor passed and their correspondence became intermittent.[50]

After Lucy's death, Jefferson wanted Polly to join him and Patsy in Europe. Jefferson's instructions to his brother-in-law demonstrates the dangers of eighteenth-century ocean travel. Polly should come over on a French or British ship to avoid possible capture by the Barbary pirates. Furthermore, the voyage should be made between April and July to avoid the hurricane season as well as a winter crossing. The ship should have made at least one round-trip Atlantic crossing but should be no more than four or five years old.[51]

While Jefferson toured southern France, he received word that Polly was on her way. He wrote Patsy the good news.

> I have received letters which inform me that our dear Polly will certainly come to us this summer. By the time I return it will be time to expect her. When she arrives, she will become a precious charge on your hands. The difference of your age, and your common loss of a mother, will put that office on you. Teach her above all things to be

50. Jefferson to Maria Cosway, Paris, October 12, 1786, and May 21, 1789, in John P. Kaminski, ed., *Jefferson in Love: The Love Letters between Thomas Jefferson & Maria Cosway* (Madison, Wis., 1999), 44, 121.

51. To Francis Eppes, August 30, 1785, *Jefferson Papers*, VIII, 451.

good: because without that we can neither be valued by others, nor set any value on ourselves. Teach her to be always true. No vice is so mean as the want of truth, & at the same time so useless. Teach her never to be angry. Anger only serves to torment ourselves, to divert others, and alienate their esteem. And teach her industry & application to useful pursuits. I will venture to assure you that if you inculcate this in her mind you will make her a happy being in herself, a most inestimable friend to you, and precious to all the world. In teaching her these dispositions of mind, you will be more fixed in them yourself, and render yourself dear to all your acquaintances. Practice them then, my dear, without ceasing. If ever you find yourself in difficulty and doubt how to extricate yourself, do what is right, & you will find it the easiest way of getting out of the difficulty. Do it for the additional incitement of increasing the happiness of him who loves you infinitely.[52]

Polly's ship stopped in England, and she and her chaperone/companion, a fourteen-year-old slave girl named Sally Hemings, stayed three weeks with John and Abigail Adams. When Polly arrived in Paris, she was enrolled in the same Catholic convent school attended by Patsy.

While in France, Jefferson enjoyed traveling through the countryside observing the people and studying agricultural practices. He wrote Lafayette that "I am never satiated with rambling through the fields and farms, examining the culture and cultivators, with a degree of curiosity which makes some take me to be a fool, and others to be much wiser than I am."[53] Jefferson was appalled by the widespread poverty in such a wealthy, fertile country. He wrote Washington that "I was much an enemy to

52. To Martha Jefferson, Toulon, April 7, 1787, ibid., XI, 278.
53. April 11, 1787, *Jefferson: Writings*, 894.

monarchy before I came to Europe. I am ten thousand times more so since I have seen what they are. There is scarcely an evil known in these countries which may not be traced to their king as its source, nor a good which is not derived from the small fibres of republicanism existing among them."[54]

Jefferson was well aware of the shortcomings of the Articles of Confederation, but his loathing for oppressive governments made him tolerant of troubling events going on in America. "I am sensible that there are defects in our federal government: yet they are so much lighter than those of monarchies that I view them with much indulgence. I rely too on the good sense of the people for remedy, whereas the evils of monarchical government are beyond remedy. If any of our countrymen wish for a king, give them Aesop's fable of the frogs who asked for a king; if this does not cure them, send them to Europe: they will go back good republicans."[55]

Divorced from the passion of the unfolding political events in America, Jefferson had few of the anxieties expressed by many of his friends. He saw uprisings like Shays's Rebellion in Massachusetts as nothing to be afraid of, and might even be a good thing:

> They are a proof that the people have liberty
> enough, and I would not wish them less than they
> have. If the happiness of the mass of the people

54. Paris, May 2, 1788, *Washington Papers*, Conf. Ser., VI, 256.

55. Jefferson to David Ramsay, Paris, August 4, 1787, *Jefferson Papers*, XI, 687. In Aesop's fable Jupiter tried to convince the frogs of a pond against having a king. When they persisted, Jupiter threw a log into their pond. The big splash awed the frogs initially, but soon they became disenchanted with their motionless sovereign. They asked for another. Jupiter sent them an eel who proved to be good natured. The frogs again wanted a more powerful monarch, whereupon Jupiter sent a heron who devoured the frogs one by one. The few survivors petitioned Jupiter for relief, but were told they were being punished for their folly and that they should have left well enough alone.

can be secured at the expense of a little tempest now & then, or even of a little blood, it will be a precious purchase. *Malo libertatum periculosum quam quietam servitutem* [I prefer dangerous liberty to a quiet servitude].[56]

To James Madison, Jefferson wrote: "I hold it that a little rebellion now and then is a good thing, & as necessary in the political world as storms in the physical. Unsuccessful rebellions indeed generally establish the encroachments on the rights of the people which have produced them. An observation of this truth should render honest republican governors so mild in their punishment of rebellions, as not to discourage them too much. It is a medicine necessary for the sound health of government."[57] To Abigail Adams he wrote: "The spirit of resistance to government is so valuable on certain occasions, that I wish it to be always kept alive. It will often be exercised when wrong, but better so than not to be exercised at all. I like a little rebellion now & then. It is like a storm in the Atmosphere."[58] To Abigail's son-in-law, Jefferson wrote that "The tree of liberty must be refreshed from time to time with the blood of patriots & tyrants. It is its natural manure."[59]

Jefferson fully supported the efforts in America to strengthen the Articles of Confederation. He was proud of his countrymen. "Happy for us, that when we find our constitutions defective & insufficient to secure the happiness of our people, we can assemble with all the coolness of philosophers & set it to rights, while every other nation on earth must have recourse to arms to amend or to restore their constitutions."[60] Jefferson characterized the Constitutional Convention meeting in Philadelphia in the spring and summer of 1787 as "an assembly of demi-gods" even though

56. To Ezra Stiles, Paris, December 24, 1786, *Jefferson Papers*, X, 629.

57. Paris, January 30, 1787, *Madison Papers*, IX, 248.

58. Paris, February 22, 1787, *Jefferson: Writings*, 889–90.

59. To William Stephens Smith, Paris, November 13, 1787, *Jefferson Papers*, XII, 356.

60. To C. W. F. Dumas, Paris, September 10, 1787, ibid., 113.

he severely criticized the delegates for holding their sessions in secret. Nothing, in Jefferson's opinion, "but the innocence of their intentions, & ignorance of the value of public discussions" could justify the "tying up of the tongues of their members."[61] A bit wary of an overreaction to the political, economic, and social instabilities racking the country, Jefferson warned that, when making constitutional revisions, "the hole & the patch should be commensurate."[62]

Jefferson admired much of what was in the new Constitution, but the lack of a bill of rights and term limits for the president and the senators concerned him greatly. He felt it best to accept the good in the Constitution and work to amend its shortcomings. When asked if he was an Antifederalist, Jefferson responded that he was

> not a Federalist, because I never submitted the whole system of my opinions to the creed of any party of men whatever in religion, in philosophy, in politics, or in anything else where I was capable of thinking for myself. Such an addiction is the last degradation of a free and moral agent. If I could not go to heaven but with a party, I would not go there at all. Therefore I protest to you I am not of the party of Federalists. But I am much farther from that of the Antifederalists.[63]

Jefferson was pleased with the outcome of the constitutional revolution in America. There was enough opposition to do good, but not enough to do bad.

Jefferson watched the constitutional revolution in America from afar. But he was much closer to the beginnings of the cataclysmic events about to explode in France and then in all of Europe. The ideology of the American Revolution had had an impact on many Frenchmen who served during that war and on the French nation as a

61. To John Adams, Paris, August 30, 1787, *Jefferson: Writings*, 908–9.

62. To James Madison, Paris, June 20, 1787, *Madison Papers*, X, 64.

63. To Francis Hopkinson, Paris, March 13, 1789, *Jefferson: Writings*, 940–41.

whole. Men like the Marquis de Lafayette led the movement for political, constitutional, economic, and social reform in France. The American ambassador discretely counseled these early French revolutionaries, cautioning slow steps and the danger from an uncontrollable mob as well as from a demagogic leader using the mob. Jefferson never wavered in his support of the French people taking control of their own government despite the brutal violence that erupted occasionally. He hoped "that the glorious example" of France would "be but the beginning of the history of European liberty."[64] He espoused the revolutionary movement while in France and continued to support it after he returned to America.

By the fall of 1788 Jefferson started appealing to Congress for a leave of absence. When Patsy announced her intention to convert to Catholicism and perhaps become a nun, Jefferson was convinced of the necessity of returning to America. He wrote President Washington on May 10, 1789, to request a leave of absence, hoping "that I may be able to get back before the winter sets in. Nothing can be so dreadful to me as to be shivering at sea for two or three months in a winter passage."[65] In June the president approved Jefferson's request.

Jefferson and his daughters left Paris on September 26, 1789, and two days later arrived at Le Havre on the French coast where they waited a week and a half before conditions allowed their passage boat to cross the channel for Cowes on the Isle of Wight. During this ten-day layover, Nathaniel Cutting, a Massachusetts merchant, spent time with the Jeffersons and described them in a journal.

> I found Mr. Jefferson a man of infinite information and sound Judgment, becoming gravity, and engaging affability mark his deportment. His

64. To Madame d'Enville, New York, April 2, 1790, ibid., 965–66.
65. Jefferson to Washington, Paris, May 10, 1789, *Washington Papers*, Pres. Ser., II, 259.

general abilities are such as would do honor to any age or Country. His eldest Daughter is an amiable Girl about 17 years of age, tall and genteel, has been 5 years in France, principally in a convent, for her Education, and though she has been so long resident in a Country remarkable for its Levity and the forward indelicacy of its manners, yet she retains all that winning simplicity, and good humored reserve that are evident proofs of innate Virtue and an happy disposition.— Characteristics which eminently distinguish the Women of America from those of any other Country. The youngest Daughter is a lovely Girl about 11 years of age. The perfect pattern of good temper, an engaging smile ever animates her Countenance, and the cheerful attention which she pays to the judicious instructions and advice of her worthy Father, the Pertinent queries which she puts to him, and the evident improvement she makes in her knowledge of Foreign Languages, History and Geography, afford a pleasing Presage that when her faculties attain their maturity, she will be the delight of her Friends, and a distinguished ornament to her sex.[66]

Another two-week delay kept them on the island before setting sail aboard the *Clermont* on October 22. Once at sea, the crossing was speedy and uneventful; "through the whole we had nothing stronger than what seamen call a stiff breeze." A relieved Jefferson could say, "I have now passed the Atlantic twice without knowing what a storm is."[67] The *Clermont* reached Norfolk, Virginia, on November 23. A month later, the family was home again at Monticello, where Jefferson pondered his future.

66. Nathaniel Cutting Journal, *Jefferson Papers*, XV, 498.

67. To William Short, Lynhaven Bay, Va., November 21, 1789, ibid., XV, 552.

SECRETARY OF STATE

When Jefferson arrived in Virginia he discovered that President Washington had nominated him as secretary of state, and the Senate had already confirmed the appointment. The state department was to have responsibility not only for foreign affairs but also for many internal matters, such as copyrights and patents, coinage, weights and measures, the census, the federal capital, certifying amendments to the Constitution, etc. With a budget of $8,000 ($3,500 for the secretary's salary) the secretary was authorized to have four clerks and a half-time translator. The president wrote Jefferson that the nomination was motivated by both "private regard" and "public propriety." Washington appreciated Jefferson's "talents and disposition" as well as his willingness to serve his country. But Washington indicated that he was "desirous to accommodate to your wishes," meaning, that if Jefferson preferred to go back to France as U.S. minister, the president would make that nomination.[68]

Jefferson responded peculiarly, neither accepting nor rejecting the nomination. Jefferson told the president that his preference was to remain as minister to France, but "it is not for an individual to choose his post. You are to marshal us as may best be for the public good." Jefferson then indicated that the final choice was Washington's. "If you think it better to transfer me to another post, my inclination must be no obstacle: nor shall it be."[69] A perplexed and somewhat annoyed Washington responded to Jefferson's ambivalence. He would not oppose Jefferson's "inclinations" to go back to France, but he felt that Jefferson was the best person to handle this difficult new assignment. That was the reason Washington made the nomination in the first place. It was, however, Jefferson's decision to make—not Washington's. In either case,

68. Washington to Jefferson, New York, October 13, 1789, *Washington Papers*, Pres. Ser., IV, 174.

69. Chesterfield, Va., December 15, 1789, ibid., 412.

Jefferson should act as quickly as possible.[70] About three weeks later, Jefferson unambiguously accepted the appointment, but indicated that he would be unable to assume the post until the end of the month. Jefferson's seventeen-year-old daughter Patsy was scheduled to marry Thomas Mann Randolph, Jr., on February 25, 1790. Jefferson felt that "the happiness of a child, for life would be hazarded were I to go away before this arrangement is made."[71]

As secretary of state, Jefferson was driven more by realpolitik than by the idealistic theorizing so characteristic of him otherwise. Two main controversies permeated Jefferson's tenure as secretary of state—America's attitude toward the French Revolution and the conflict between Jefferson and Secretary of the Treasury Alexander Hamilton over the kind of government and economy best suited for the United States.

Jefferson came back from Europe a firm supporter of the French Revolution. He believed it the harbinger of liberty throughout Europe and a valuable support to the still tenuous American experiment in republicanism. Should the French fail to establish a firm, free, republican government, European freedom would suffer a decisive blow and Americans might find their own Constitution "falling back to that kind of a Half-way house, the English constitution."[72]

As France and Britain came into conflict, Secretary Jefferson lobbied President Washington in support of the French; Secretary Hamilton—whose economic policies depended on the duties from British trade—in support of the British. The president tried to keep America neutral, believing that the country should not risk the consequences of involvement in a European war. Hamilton

70. Washington to Jefferson, New York, January 21, 1790, ibid., V, 29–31.

71. Jefferson to Washington and to Madison, Monticello, both February 14, 1790, ibid., 138, 165n.

72. To George Mason, Philadelphia, February 4, 1791, *Jefferson: Writings*, 971–72.

strenuously opposed war with Britain and any discriminatory commercial legislation against Britain even though that country discriminated against America. Hamilton's economic policy was based largely upon revenue derived from duties on goods imported primarily from Britain. Any anti-British policy would endanger that revenue stream. Jefferson also realized that American involvement in a European war would be disastrous, but did not support neutrality, which violated America's treaty commitments to France. He pointed out the importance of France to America in case war broke out with either Spain or Britain. Washington agreed that the U.S. should cultivate closer relations with France, including the resumption of debt payments, which Hamilton had urged be suspended. This, according to Jefferson, "was the very doctrine which had been my polar star."[73] Jefferson accordingly instructed Gouverneur Morris, U.S. minister to France, that the United States "desire[s] the closest union" with France. "Mutual good offices, mutual affection and similar principles of government seem to have destined the two peoples for the most intimate communion, and even for a complete exchange of citizenship among the individuals composing them."[74] Jefferson advocated the doctrine that the United States would recognize any functioning government: "We surely cannot deny to any nation that right whereon our government is founded."[75] It was imperative, Jefferson believed, to get this principle on the "record in the letter books of my office."[76]

In January 1793, Jefferson wrote his former personal secretary William Short (who had been elevated to chargé

73. Notes of a Conversation with George Washington on Foreign Affairs, December 27, 1792, ibid., XXIV, 793.

74. Philadelphia, December 30, 1792, ibid., 801.

75. Ibid., 800.

76. Notes on the Legitimacy of Government, December 30, 1792, ibid., 802.

d'affaires to France when Jefferson became secretary of state) to stop sending reports vividly describing the brutality of the Reign of Terror in France. Jefferson believed, as he told Lafayette, "We are not to expect to be translated from despotism to liberty in a feather bed."[77] Short's reports undermined Jefferson in his struggles with Secretary Hamilton, both in foreign affairs and domestic matters. In dramatic language Jefferson told Short how important the French Revolution was to the world in general and to the United States in particular. The unjust deaths of a few must be weighed against the benefits to be derived.

> In the struggle which was necessary, many guilty persons fell without the forms of trial, and with them some innocent. These I deplore as much as any body, & shall deplore some of them to the day of my death. But I deplore them as I should have done had they fallen in battle. It was necessary to use the arm of the people, a machine not quite so blind as balls and bombs, but blind to a certain degree. A few of their cordial friends met at their hands the fate of enemies. But time and truth will rescue & embalm their memories, while their posterity will be enjoying that very liberty for which they would never have hesitated to offer up their lives. The liberty of the whole earth was depending on the issue of the contest, and was ever such a prize won with so little innocent blood? My own affections have been deeply wounded by some of the martyrs to this cause, but rather than it should have failed, I would have seen half the earth desolated. Were there but an Adam & Eve left in every country, & left free, it would be better than as it is now.[78]

77. Jefferson to Lafayette, New York, April 2, 1790, ibid., XVI, 293.
78. Philadelphia, January 3, 1793, *Jefferson: Writings*, 1004.

Jefferson believed that Hamilton sought to reestablish monarchy in America and that Hamilton's economic plan would create a favored class dominated by Northern merchants and speculators. Jefferson opposed the creation of the Bank of the United States ostensibly on constitutional grounds. In reality, Jefferson's objection was more pragmatic. Modeled on the Bank of England, the Bank of the United States would ally the federal government with wealthy (largely Northern) shareholders who would reap windfall dividends when the bank loaned its capital to large merchants in preference to small farmers—at high rates of interest. The payment of the federal debt (largely now in the hands of Northern speculators) at face value and the assumption of the states' wartime debts by the federal government would also bountifully benefit this favored class. Hamilton's Report on Manufactures, which proposed bounties and subsidies to private individuals, was even more blatantly unconstitutional and corrupt in the sense of favoring only one part of society.

To counteract Hamilton's policies, which Jefferson said had given rise to the formation of a political party, Jefferson and James Madison led the movement to create an organized opposition. "Our citizens are divided into two political sects. One which fears the people most, the other the government."[79] Jefferson justified the creation of the Republican Party and his involvement in it.

> The same political parties which now agitate the U.S. have existed thro' all time. Whether the power of the people, or that of the aristocrats should prevail, were questions which kept the states of Greece & Rome in eternal convulsions; as they now schismatize every people whose minds and mouths are not shut up by the gag of a despot.[80]

79. Jefferson to Count de Volney, Monticello, December 9, 1795, *Jefferson Papers*, XXVIII, 551.

80. To John Adams, Monticello, June 27, 1813, *Adams-Jefferson Letters*, 335.

Unlike the political parties of Great Britain, the Republican Party was not created out of "a greediness for office. . . . Where the principle of difference is as substantial and as strongly pronounced as between the republicans & the Monocrats of our country I hold it as honorable to take a firm & decided part, and as immoral to pursue a middle line, as between the parties of Honest men, & Rogues, into which every country is divided."[81]

As secretary of state, Jefferson continued the long-standing difficult negotiations with Spain over the right of Americans freely to navigate the Mississippi River and to transfer their agricultural produce from flat-bottom river boats to ocean-going vessels. Writing to the American chargé d'affaires in Madrid, Jefferson used the threat of western violence for leverage.

> It is impossible to answer for the forbearance of our Western citizens. We endeavor to quiet them with the expectation of an attainment of their rights by peaceable means. But should they in a moment of impatience hazard others, there is no saying how far we may be led; for neither themselves nor their rights will ever be abandoned by us.[82]

Spain heightened tensions between the two countries by arming and inciting the Creeks and other Indians in the Southwest Territory. Jefferson felt that by not meddling in European politics, America could avoid hostilities. But if provoked, America would respond with "firmness," regardless of the cost. If Spain persisted in inciting the Creeks, America would annihilate them and go to war with Spain as well, "with regret, but without fear."[83]

81. To William Branch Giles, Monticello, December 31, 1795, *Jefferson Papers*, XXVIII, 566.

82. To William Carmichael, New York, August 2, 1790, ibid., XVII, 112.

83. To William Carmichael and William Short, Philadelphia, June 30, 1793, ibid., XXVI, 411.

Jefferson also denounced the British policy of arming
and inciting the Indians of the Old Northwest Territory.
United tribes had badly defeated an American military
expedition in 1789. Jefferson expected that a new expedition under Governor Arthur St. Clair in the summer of
1791 would "give them a thorough drubbing." After that,
Jefferson believed we should "bribe them into peace, and
to retain them in peace by eternal bribes."[84]

Jefferson had long believed that "The two principles
on which our conduct towards the Indians should be
founded are justice & fear. After the injuries we have done
them, they cannot love us, which leaves us no alternative
but that of fear to keep them from attacking us. But
justice is what we should never lose sight of, & in time it
may recover their esteem."[85] Eventually Jefferson came to
believe that the only choice for Indian peoples was to
assimilate into the white man's society.

> In truth, the ultimate point of rest & happiness
> for them is to let our settlements and theirs meet
> and blend together, to intermix and become one
> people, incorporating themselves with us as citi-
> zens of the U.S. This is what the natural progress
> of things will of course bring on, and it will be
> better to promote than to retard it. Surely it will
> be better for them to be identified with us, and
> preserved in the occupation of their lands, than
> be exposed to the many casualties which may
> endanger them while a separate people.[86]

84. To Charles Carroll of Carrollton, Philadelphia, April 15, 1791,
Jefferson: Writings, 977. St. Clair's expedition was almost annihilated in
November 1791. Anthony Wayne defeated the Indians at Fallen Timbers
in 1794.

85. To Benjamin Hawkins, Paris, August 13, 1786, *Jefferson Papers*,
X, 240.

86. To Benjamin Hawkins, Washington, February 18, 1803, *Jefferson:
Writings*, 1115.

THE SECOND RETIREMENT

Soon after Washington was elected to a second term as president, Jefferson announced his intention to resign. He delayed it once, but at the end of 1793, after spending nearly half of his life in public service, the fifty-year-old Jefferson retired to Monticello for a second time, hoping this time to remain forever a private citizen. His debt of service had "been fully & faithfully paid." He admitted that there was a time

> when perhaps the esteem of the world was of higher value in my eye than everything in it. But age, experience & reflection, preserving to that only its due value, have set a higher on tranquility. The motion of my blood no longer keeps time with the tumult of the world. It leads me to seek for happiness in the lap and love of my family, in the society of my neighbors & my books, in the wholesome occupations of my farm & my affairs, in an interest or affection in every bud that opens, in every breath that blows around me, in an entire freedom of rest or motion, of thought or incogitancy, owing account to myself alone of my hours & actions.[87]

He wrote Vice President Adams that

> I return to farming with an ardor which I scarcely knew in my youth, and which has got the better entirely of my love of study. Instead of writing 10 or 12 letters a day, which I have been in the habit of doing as a thing of course, I put off answering my letters now, farmer-like, till a rainy day, & then find it sometimes postponed by other necessary occupations.[88]

87. To James Madison, June 9, 1793, *Jefferson: Writings*, 1009–10.
88. Monticello, April 25, 1794, *Adams-Jefferson Letters*, 254.

To Secretary of War Henry Knox he wrote "I am become the most ardent farmer in the state. I live on my horse from morning to night almost."[89]

The plantation—both fields and buildings—were dilapidated and needed his full attention. Jefferson reorganized his holdings into six rotation patterns. Because the farming was temporarily a financial drain, Jefferson started a nailery employing a dozen young male slaves. The factory soon produced a ton and a half of nails a month, which Jefferson sold to storekeepers and planters or kept for his own use. Supervising the business himself, it yielded "a profit on which I can get along till I can put my farms into a course of yielding profit."[90] Ever experimenting, he applied "mathematical principles" to a new design for a mould-board plow that brought added efficiencies to farming and won awards for him from various agricultural societies at home and abroad.[91] He continued collecting and compiling the ancient and modern laws of Virginia, hoping that a new printed compilation would preserve this valuable legal and historical heritage.[92] He immediately set to work "repairing, altering & finishing" his residence—a work already twenty-five years in the making with another twenty-five years of work still to come.[93]

But Jefferson could never totally abandon the outside world. Although he cancelled his newspaper subscriptions and read few pamphlets, national and international news still flowed to Monticello through the rivers of correspondence from abroad and from politically active friends in America who wanted him back in the fray.

89. Monticello, August 30, 1795, Knox Papers, Gilder-Lehrman Collection, New-York Historical Society.

90. To Jean Nicolas Démeunier, Monticello, April 29, 1795, *Jefferson: Writings*, 1028–29.

91. To John Taylor, Monticello, December 29, 1794, ibid., 1021–22.

92. To George Wythe, Monticello, January 16, 1796, ibid., 1031–32.

93. To Count de Volney, Monticello, April 10, 1796, *Jefferson Papers*, XXIX, 61.

In the years of his retirement, Jefferson became increasingly convinced that the central government's policies were more than ever under the control of the monarchist Hamilton. When, in September 1796, President Washington announced his decision to retire after the completion of his second term, it became obvious to Republicans that they needed a candidate to run for president who would combat the dangerous tendency of amassing power in the central government and the growing subservience to Great Britain. At first Jefferson was determined not to run: "I would not give up my own retirement for the empire of the universe."[94] Jefferson wanted James Madison to do it, but everyone knew that only Jefferson stood a chance to defeat John Adams. Jefferson relented. Hoping to preserve republicanism in America from the machinations of Alexander Hamilton and other monarchists and lovers of Britain, Jefferson agreed not to decline the presidency.

Jefferson's candidacy did not come as a surprise to many of his opponents. They distrusted him and felt that his retirement from the state department was politically motivated. Years later Adams described the attitude toward Jefferson in the mid–1790s.

Jefferson resigned his office as Secretary of State and retired, and his friends said he had struck a great stroke to obtain the presidency. . . . The whole anti-Federal party at that time considered this retirement as a sure and certain step towards the summit of the pyramid and, accordingly, represented him as unambitious, unavaricious, and perfectly disinterested in all parts of all the states in the union. When a man has one of the two greatest parties in a nation interested in representing him to be disinterested, even those who

94. To James Madison, Monticello, December 28, 1794, *Jefferson: Writings*, 1017.

believe it to be a lie will repeat it so often to one another that at last they will seem to believe it to be true. Jefferson has succeeded; and multitudes are made to believe that he is pure benevolence; that he desires no profit; that he wants no patronage; that if you will only let him govern, he will rule only to make the people happy. But you and I know him to be an intriguer.[95]

Alexander Hamilton felt that it was critical that Washington's "successor shall be a safe man." It was less important who that person was, as long as "it shall not be Jefferson. We have every thing to fear if this man comes in." Federalists must work together—set aside all "personal and partial considerations . . . to give to the great object of excluding Jefferson."[96]

As was the custom of the day, neither Adams nor Jefferson campaigned. With the country sorely divided, many, including Jefferson, thought that no candidate would receive a majority of the electoral votes and that the election would then revert to the House of Representatives. In such a case, Jefferson preferred that Adams be elected because of his seniority. "He has always been my senior, from the commencement of our public life, and the expression of the public will being equal, this circumstance ought to give him the preference." Jefferson wrote to Madison that "there is nothing I so anxiously hope, as that my name may come out either second or third."[97] The electoral vote was close, and both Adams and Jefferson received majorities of the electoral vote—73

95. Adams to Benjamin Rush, September 1807, John A. Schutz and Douglas Adair, eds., *The Spur of Fame: Dialogues of John Adams and Benjamin Rush, 1805–1813* (reprint ed., Indianapolis, n.d.), 101.

96. From Alexander Hamilton, New York, November 8, 1796, Harold C. Syrett, ed., *The Papers of Alexander Hamilton* (27 vols., New York, 1961–1987), XX, 376–77.

97. To James Madison, Monticello, December 17, 1796, *Madison Papers*, XVI, 431.

to 68. Adams would be president and Jefferson vice president. Jefferson was pleased. He hoped that Adams could "be induced to administer the government on its true principles, & to relinquish his bias to an English constitution." Furthermore it might be beneficial for the country if Adams and the Republicans would work together in future elections. "He is perhaps the only sure barrier against Hamilton's getting in."[98]

As vice president, Jefferson believed that he would not be an executive officer. He would not attend cabinet meetings, but would only preside over the Senate. Jefferson wrote that "the second office of this government is honorable & easy, the first is but a splendid misery."[99] Jefferson thanked Benjamin Rush

> for your congratulations on the public call on me to undertake the second office in the United States, but still more for the justice you do me in viewing as I do the escape from the first. I have no wish to meddle again in public affairs. . . . If I am to act however, a more tranquil and unoffending station could not have been found for me. . . . It will give me philosophical evenings in the winter, and rural days in summer.[100]

THE REIGN OF WITCHES

When John Adams became president in 1797, he faced a crisis in foreign affairs. The recently adopted Jay Treaty did little to improve Anglo-American relations, but it convinced France that America, with its pro-British president, was siding with its inveterate enemy. France refused

98. Jefferson to James Madison, Monticello, January 1, 1797, *Jefferson: Writings*, 1039.

99. To Elbridge Gerry, Philadelphia, May 13, 1797, *Jefferson Papers*, XXIX, 362.

100. To Benjamin Rush, Monticello, January 22, 1797, ibid., 275.

to accept America's new minister, and French warships began seizing American merchantmen.

In his opening speech to the Senate, Jefferson praised Adams as an American patriot. Adams suggested to Jefferson that James Madison might be appointed minister to France to repair the diplomatic damage; but before Jefferson could deliver Madison's refusal of the appointment, the president had already taken the advice of his cabinet and withdrawn the offer. From this moment Adams turned a cold shoulder to Jefferson, never seeking his advice.

Adams called a special session of Congress and delivered what Republicans perceived as a war message that elevated the country's passions against France. Another American peace initiative failed when France refused either to accept America's ambassador or to negotiate unless a bribe was first provided. France and America went to war at sea. Congress voted to expand the navy and provide for a provisional army of 25,000 to defend against a potential French invasion. President Adams asked George Washington to come out of retirement and be commander-in-chief of the army. Washington accepted on the condition that Alexander Hamilton be second in command. Reluctantly Adams accepted Washington's terms. Jefferson perceived the danger of a powerful, oppressive army led in the field by a power hungry monarchist like Hamilton.

With war raging in Europe, many Europeans emigrated to America. Most were sympathetic to the Republicans. In an effort to silence the ever growing criticism of the administration, Congress passed and the president signed a new Naturalization Act, Alien acts, and the Sedition Act. The Naturalization Act and the Alien acts made it harder to become citizens and easier for the president to deport aliens from both friendly and enemy countries. (Adams never used the Alien acts.) The Sedition Act provided that anyone who criticized the president or Congress (the vice president was not mentioned) could be prosecuted and, if found guilty, fined and imprisoned. The federal judiciary—all Federalists—enthusiastically enforced the Sedition Act and several Republican printers and congressmen were imprisoned and fined.

Republicans were convinced of the unconstitutionality of the Alien and Sedition laws. Secretly, Jefferson wrote a series of resolutions condemning the acts. Jefferson asserted that the states had united and formed a compact creating a central government with strictly limited powers. The Sedition Act went far beyond the federal government's power and thus could be nullified by the states. In December 1798, the Kentucky legislature adopted Jefferson's resolutions but only after making significant modifications eliminating the reference to nullification. James Madison wrote similar resolutions, though he never advocated nullification, which were adopted by the Virginia legislature in November 1798. No other state endorsed the states' rights position espoused in the Virginia and Kentucky resolutions.

Despite various appeals for a division of the Union, Jefferson cautioned against such extremes. Federalist and New England domination were only temporary. The popularity of Washington and "the cunning of Hamilton" had deceived men who would normally be Republicans. "Time alone would bring around an order of things more correspondent to the sentiments of our constituents." War, taxes, and violations of the Constitution would have their impact. "A little patience, and we shall see the reign of witches pass over, their spells dissolve, and the people, recovering their true sight, restore their government to its true principles." Who could say whether a divided America would be an improvement. Better to maintain the Union and separate totally from Europe. If Americans felt European power just enough "to hoop us together, it will be the happiest situation in which we can exist."[101]

Realizing that war with America was terribly unwise, the French government sent out peace feelers. Although President Adams was riding a wave of popularity because of the war hysteria, Adams responded positively to the French overtures by sending a new diplomatic delegation to France to avert war, much to the disgust of many fellow Federalists. This effort to achieve peace exposed the deep fissure among Federalists. The Hamilton wing of the party condemned the president and hoped to defeat both Adams and Jefferson in the upcoming presidential election of 1800.

THE REVOLUTION OF 1800

In 1800, Republicans sensed a real opportunity to win control of the presidency and both houses of Congress. The country was so evenly divided that it seemed likely the presidential election would be determined by whoever received the electoral votes of New York, which were chosen by the legislature. The New York legislature was so evenly divided that whichever party won the New York City election would have a majority, and with that would receive all of the state's electoral votes.

Aaron Burr, who had been the Republican candidate for vice president in 1796, developed a masterful strategy for the election of New York City assemblymen, and in the spring of 1800 Republicans elected their candidates. It was widely assumed that unless something unforeseen happened, Jefferson would be elected president in the fall. For his efforts, Burr expected and received the endorsement of the Republican congressional caucus as vice president. Remembering that the 1796 Virginia presidential electors had cast their ballots for Samuel Adams instead of for him, Burr demanded that no electoral votes should

101. To John Taylor, Philadelphia, June 4, 1798, *Jefferson: Writings*, 1050. "To hoop us together" referred to the use of hoops to keep the staves of a barrel together.

be diverted away from him in 1800. A grateful Jefferson, Madison, and the rest of the republican leadership agreed.

The presidential election of 1800 was unbelievably virulent. Jefferson was vilified as a Jacobin who would plunge America into a reign of terror, as an atheist slave-owner who would destroy the country's morals, and as an ally of France who would involve America in the carnage of European war. Federalists saw Jefferson as "too theoretical & fanciful a statesman to direct with steadiness & prudence the affairs of this extensive & growing confederacy."[102] Hamilton outwardly supported the Federalist ticket of President Adams and Charles Cotesworth Pinckney of South Carolina, but secretly campaigned for Pinckney to unseat Adams.

Jefferson and Burr each received 73 electoral votes, while Adams received 65 votes and Pinckney 64. Republicans decisively won almost a two-thirds majority of the new House of Representatives. But with Jefferson and Burr tied (and having a majority of the electoral votes), the choice between the two Republican candidates was to be decided by the lame-duck House of Representatives controlled by Federalists. Voting by state delegations, the House was split with eight states favoring Jefferson, six for Burr, and two divided. Neither Jefferson nor Burr made any quid pro quo deals, but neither did Burr explicitly renounce a willingness to be elected president. Hamilton vigorously supported Jefferson, indicating in his correspondence with Federalist representatives that the "*profligate*" Burr had no scruples and could never be trusted to fulfill any promise. Hamilton also discounted much of the Federalist campaign rhetoric about Jefferson. As much as Hamilton personally disliked Jefferson, he recognized that the Virginian would accept certain practical political constraints. Hamilton wrote to Delaware's lone representative, James A. Bayard, who leaned toward Burr:

102. Charles Carroll of Carrollton to Alexander Hamilton, Annapolis, April 18, 1800, *Hamilton Papers*, XXIV, 412.

Nor is it true that Jefferson is zealot enough to do anything in pursuance of his principles which will contravene his popularity, or his interest. He is as likely as any man I know to temporize—to calculate what will be likely to promote his own reputation and advantage; and the probable result of such a temper is the preservation of systems, though originally opposed, which being once established, could not be overturned without danger to the person who did it. To my mind a true estimate of Mr. J's. character warrants the expectation of a temporizing rather than a violent system. That Jefferson has manifested a culpable predilection for France is certainly true; but I think it a question whether it did not proceed quite as much from her *popularity* among us, as from sentiment, and in proportion as that popularity is diminished his zeal will cool. Add to this that there is no fair reason to suppose him capable of being corrupted, which is a security that he will not go beyond certain limits.[103]

The House began voting on February 16, only three weeks before the anticipated inauguration. Finally, after thirty-six ballots, Bayard submitted a blank ballot, removing Delaware from the Burr column. South Carolina also voted blank, and the only Republican in the Vermont delegation cast the state's vote for Jefferson. Ten states voted for Jefferson, four for Burr, and two voted blank. Jefferson was elected without a single Federalist vote. Years later Jefferson referred to the election as "the revolution of 1800—as real a revolution in the principles of our government as that of 1776."[104]

103. New York, January 16, 1801, *Hamilton Papers*, XXV, 320.
104. To Spencer Roane, Poplar Forest, September 6, 1819, *Jefferson: Writings*, 1425.

PRESIDENT

March 4, 1801, is an important day in American history, in the history of freedom. On this day power was transferred peacefully from one political party to an opposing party. The 57-year-old president-elect walked from his boardinghouse to the unfinished Capitol virtually indistinguishable from his fellow citizens. At Jefferson's request, Chief Justice John Marshall (a distant cousin and staunch political opponent) administered the oath of office. The luster of the event was tarnished only slightly because of the absence of the outgoing president—John Adams had left the city at 4:00 that morning. Although Jefferson and Adams would live another quarter century, they would never see each other again. In fact, for the next ten years they remained estranged.

Jefferson's inaugural address, spoken in his soft, almost inaudible voice in the Senate chamber overcrowded with 1,000 people, is one of the great documents in American political literature. Knowing that reconciliation was desperately needed, the new president offered an outstretched open hand. "Every difference of opinion is not a difference of principle. We have called by different names brethren of principle. We are all Republicans, we are all Federalists." He reminded Federalists and Republicans alike that though the "sacred principle" of majority rule "is in all cases to prevail, that will to be rightful must be reasonable; that the minority possess their equal rights, which equal law must protect, and to violate would be oppression." He pleaded with his countrymen to "unite with one heart and one mind" to restore "harmony and affection" to their social intercourse. "The honor, the happiness, and the hopes of this beloved country" were dependent on their actions. In a brief two-minute statement, he outlined "the essential principles of our Government," which would be the general policies of his administration.

Equal and exact justice to all men, of whatever state or persuasion, religious or political; peace, commerce, and honest friendship with all nations, entangling alliances with none; the support of the State governments in all their rights, as the most competent administrations for our domestic concerns and the surest bulwarks against antirepublican tendencies; the preservation of the General Government in its whole constitutional vigor, as the sheet anchor of our peace at home and safety abroad; a jealous care of the right of election by the people—a mild and safe corrective of abuses which are lopped by the sword of revolution where peaceable remedies are unprovided; absolute acquiescence in the decisions of the majority, the vital principle of republics, from which is no appeal but to force, the vital principle and immediate parent of despotism; a well-disciplined militia, our best reliance in peace and for the first moments of war till regulars may relieve them; the supremacy of the civil over the military authority; economy in the public expense, that labor may be lightly burthened; the honest payment of our debts and sacred preservation of the public faith; encouragement of agriculture, and of commerce as its handmaid; the diffusion of information and arraignment of all abuses at the bar of the public reason; freedom of religion; freedom of the press, and freedom of person under the protection of the habeas corpus, and trial by juries impartially selected.[105]

Jefferson wanted to establish a new, more republican, image as president. His wardrobe as president might best be described as frumpy. Like Washington, he understood the importance of image and precedent. He chose to cul-

105. March 4, 1801, *Jefferson: Writings*, 492–96.

tivate a more common image. He hated the tapestry of monarchy and through dress and action attempted to abandon the old ways in favor of the new.

At his inauguration he wore no sword. For two weeks after the inauguration he resided and dined in a public boardinghouse. He rode around the city of Washington not in a coach, but on horseback. He wore no powdered wig and he sometimes answered the door of the president's house in his robe and slippers or in "old-fashioned clothes, which were not in the nicest order, or of the most elegant kind." At state dinners guests sat pell-mell instead of according to the rigid standards of diplomatic protocol. He replaced the weekly formal levees with informal dinners three or four times weekly with a dozen or so members of Congress at a time. He stopped holding celebrations of his birthday and sent his annual messages to Congress in writing rather than addressing them personally. He made himself accessible to and familiar with the people. In personal meetings he was "a little awkward in his first address, but you are immediately at ease in his presence. His manners are inviting and not uncourtly; and his voice flexible and distinct. He bears the marks of intense thought and perseverance in his countenance. . . . His smile is very engaging and impresses you with cheerful frankness. His familiarity, however, is tempered with great calmness of manner and with becoming propriety. Open to all, he seems willing to stand the test of inquiry, and to be weighed in the balance only by his merit and attainments."[106] This lack of formality and openness was not merely a matter of style or political expediency. This was how Jefferson liked to live.

But when the occasion required, Jefferson could present a completely different, more formal image. Federalist Senator William Plumer of New Hampshire described one of Jefferson's congressional dinners composed of two

106. The quotations in this paragraph are taken from Joseph Story to Samuel P. P. Fay, Washington, May 30, 1807, William W. Story, ed., *Life and Letters of Joseph Story* (2 vols., Boston, 1851), I, 151–52.

senators, ten representatives (including Jefferson's two sons-in-law), and his private secretary. The president "was well dressed—A new suit of black—silk hose—shoes—clean linen, & his hair highly powdered." The dinner "was elegant & rich—his wines very good—there were eight different kinds of which there were rich Hungary, & still richer *Tokay*."[107] No toasts were made either during or after dinner so that guests could limit their consumption. Jefferson also had "on the table two bottles of water brought from the river Mississippi, & a quantity of the Mammoth cheese. This cheese, was one made by some Democrats in Massachusetts two three years since, & presented to Mr. Jefferson. It weighed 1200 lb. & is very far from being good."[108] The president's table had "a great variety of pies, fruit & nuts." He served ice cream balls placed between warmed pastry. Jefferson "performed the honors of the table with great facility—He was reserved—appeared rather low spirited—conversed little—he is naturally very social & communicative." Plumer noticed that "when dinner is announced the president "directs the company to walk, & he is the last that enters the dining room."[109] Another frequent dinner guest, New York Senator Samuel L. Mitchill wrote that Jefferson "is tall in stature and rather spare in flesh. His dress and manners are very plain; he is grave, or rather sedate, but

107. Jefferson told Plumer that the Tokay had cost a guinea a bottle which was but slightly larger than a quart.

108. The mammoth cheese (four feet wide in diameter, fifteen inches thick, and weighing 1235 lbs.) was made in the summer of 1801 by the Baptist congregation of Cheshire, Mass., allegedly from the milk of 900 Republican cows. It was transported down the Hudson River on a sloop to Baltimore and then by a wagon drawn by six horses and was presented to Jefferson as part of the customary New Year's day gifts. It was inscribed: "The greatest cheese in America—for the greatest man in America." Because Jefferson opposed this monarchical custom of giving gifts, he made a $200 donation to the congregation (considerably more than the retail price of the cheese).

109. *Plumer's Memorandum*, December 3, 1805, 212–13.

without any tincture of pomp, ostentation, or pride, and occasionally can smile, and both hear and relate humorous stories as well as any other man of social feelings."[110]

Jefferson's determination to be conciliatory was tested immediately. Federalists feared that the president would yield to the demands of partisan Republicans who wanted all Federalist officeholders replaced with Republicans. Instead, Jefferson vowed to retain qualified officeholders who were doing a good job. Only incompetent officials, those who were overtly partisan, and those appointed by President Adams during his lame-duck last two months would be removed. For the most part Jefferson stuck to his policy, and therefore he satisfied neither Federalists nor the more ardent wing of his own party. With the aim of redressing the imbalance in federal service, Jefferson filled all vacancies with Republicans.

Within weeks of taking office, Jefferson developed a policy of not responding to office seekers. The answer to a job solicitation would "be found in what is done or not done."[111] Applicants would be informed "by the fact."[112] If you received a commission, you knew that you got the appointment; with no commission, you could be assured that someone else had been nominated. Toward the end of his presidency, Jefferson explained the difficulty of making appointments. Throughout his tenure, Jefferson found that

solicitations for office are the most painful incidents to which an Executive magistrate is

110. To Mrs. Mitchill, Washington, January 10, 1802, "Dr. Mitchill's Letters from Washington: 1801–1813," *Harper's New Monthly Magazine*, 58 (1879), 743.

111. Jefferson to Aaron Burr, Washington, November 18, 1801, Mary-Jo Kline, ed., *Political Correspondence and Public Papers of Aaron Burr* (2 vols., Princeton, 1983), II, 637.

112. Jefferson to Larkin Smith, Washington, November 26, 1804, Jefferson Papers, Library of Congress.

exposed. The ordinary affairs of a nation offer little difficulty to a person of any experience; but the gift of office is the dreadful burden which oppresses him. A person who wishes to make it an engine of self-elevation, may do wonders with it; but to one who wishes to use it conscientiously for the public good, without regard to the ties of blood or friendship, it creates enmities without number, many open, but more secret, and saps the happiness and peace of his life.[113]

His policy was "to make the best appointment my information & judgment enable me to do, & then fold myself up in the mantle of conscience & abide unmoved by the peltings of the storm."[114]

Jefferson's policy of retaining most officeholders did not extend to the "midnight appointments" made by President Adams during his lame-duck months. The outgoing Federalist Congress passed the Judiciary Act of 1801, which created sixteen new circuit courts (one for each state) each with its own lifetime judge as well as the whole panoply of court officials (clerks, bailiffs, marshals, reporters, etc.). All of Adams's appointments were Federalists—many of them overtly partisan. Since federal judges could not be removed, Jefferson worked with Congress to repeal the Judiciary Act of 1801 and replace it with the Judiciary Act of 1802, which, according to Jefferson, dismissed no judge directly, but simply eliminated the courts. The Supreme Court wrestled with the constitutionality of this action, and reluctantly acquiesced.

Jefferson's conflict with the federal judiciary continued. When the Constitution was first proposed, Jefferson opposed the omission of a bill of rights because he wanted such a declaration to be used by judges as a "legal check" in defense of liberty. The independence of the

113. To Governor James Sullivan, Washington, March 3, 1808, Washington, *Jefferson Writings*, V, 252.

114. To Benjamin Rush, Washington, January 3, 1808, ibid., 225.

judiciary, Jefferson felt, "merits great confidence for their learning and integrity."[115] However judges in the 1790s had not protected rights but had become instruments of partisan oppression, especially in prosecuting cases under the Sedition Act. One of Jefferson's first acts as president was to pardon all those convicted under the Sedition Act. He then encouraged the House of Representatives to impeach New Hampshire federal judge John Pickering, who was alcoholic, insane, and partisan while presiding over cases. The Senate convicted and removed Pickering. Because of the difficulty of impeaching and convicting judges, Jefferson favored a constitutional amendment to remove judges by address—removal by the president upon the request of both houses of Congress.[116] When that amendment failed to move forward, Jefferson encouraged the House to impeach Samuel Chase, an associate justice of the U.S. Supreme Court. For whatever reason, Jefferson seems not to have pursued the impeachment, possibly because Secretary of State James Madison and Secretary of the Treasury Albert Gallatin convinced him of the impropriety of making the judiciary subservient to the other two branches of government. A majority of the Senate voted to convict Chase on only two of the eight charges against him, not the two-thirds majority needed for removal. The full-scale attack on judges ended here, although Jefferson would have a lifelong animosity for the federal courts, led by Chief Justice Marshall. Jefferson complained that "The constitution . . . is a mere thing of wax in the hands of the judiciary, which they may twist and shape into any form they please."[117] According to Jefferson:

115. Jefferson to James Madison, Paris, March 15, 1789, *Jefferson Papers*, XIV, 659.

116. *Plumer's Memorandum*, January 7, 1804, p. 102. Removal of judges by address was part of the English system. It had been proposed and rejected in the Constitutional Convention of 1787.

117. To Spencer Roane, Poplar Forest, September 6, 1819, *Jefferson: Writings*, 1426.

the germ of dissolution of our federal government is in the constitution of the federal judiciary; an irresponsible body (for impeachment is scarcely a scare-crow), working like gravity by night and by day, gaining a little to-day & a little to-morrow, and advancing its noiseless step like a thief, over the field of jurisdiction, until all shall be usurped from the states, & the government of all be consolidated into one.[118]

Chief Justice Marshall had his own theory to explain Jefferson's attitude toward the judiciary. "The great Lama of the mountains," [119] as Marshall called Jefferson,

is among the most ambitious, & I suspect among the most unforgiving of men. His great power is over the mass of the people & this power is chiefly acquired by professions of democracy. Every check on the wild impulse of the moment is a check on his own power, & he is unfriendly to the source from which it flows. He looks, of course, with ill will at an independent judiciary.

That in a free country with a written constitution, any intelligent man should wish a dependent judiciary, or should think that the constitution is not a law for the court as well as the legislature, would astonish me if I had not learnt from observation that, with many men, the judgment is completely controlled by the passions.[120]

By the 1820s, according to Marshall, there was

118. To Charles Hammond, Monticello, August 18, 1821, Washington, *Jefferson Writings*, VII, 216.

119. John Marshall to Joseph Story, Richmond, September 18, 1821, Herbert A. Johnson et al., eds., *The Papers of John Marshall* (11 vols. to date, Williamsburg, Va., 1974–), IX, 183.

120. Marshall to Joseph Story, Richmond, July 13, 1821, ibid., 179.

A deep design to convert our government into a mere league of States. . . . The attack upon the judiciary is in fact an attack upon the union. The judicial department is well understood to be that through which the government may be attacked most successfully, because it is without patronage, & of course without power, and it is equally well understood that every subtraction from its jurisdiction is a vital wound to the government itself. The attack upon it therefore is a marked battery aimed at the government itself. The whole attack, if not originating with Mr. Jefferson, is obviously approved & guided by him.[121]

Jefferson felt that his most important action as president would be to pay off the federal debt. Secretary Hamilton believed that a national debt was a blessing in that it tied the interest of the creditors to the central government; Jefferson believed that a national debt was a source of corruption and an evil that required high taxes to pay interest and principal to a favored class of citizen.

Albert Gallatin, Jefferson's secretary of the treasury, devised a program to retire the entire federal debt in sixteen years. After eliminating virtually all federal domestic taxes, Gallatin estimated annual revenue at $9 million from duties on imported goods and the sale of government land. Gallatin proposed that $7 million annually be earmarked to paying the debt. This left $2 million for the annual cost of government. The army was reduced to garrison duty on the frontier, much of the navy was decommissioned and sold off, and the civil list was held stable. When Jefferson took office the federal government employed only 127 people in the capital. When he retired in 1809, even with the doubling of the size of the country,

121. Marshall to Joseph Story, Richmond, September 18, 1821, ibid., 184.

only 123 people served in Washington, D.C. With commerce greatly expanding, Gallatin's revenue estimates were regularly exceeded and by 1806 the government was running a surplus beyond its scheduled payment of the debt. To assist Gallatin, Jefferson pragmatically kept the Bank of the United States functioning because it served a useful purpose in handling the government's money. Gallatin, however, did sell all of the government's stock in the bank.

Foreign affairs threatened Jefferson's austerity program. In 1801 the pasha of Tripoli, one of the Barbary states, again attacked and captured American merchantmen. As in the mid-1780s, Jefferson felt that the best way to handle this attack was with a show of military force. Unsanctioned by Congress, he sent a small fleet to the Mediterranean with instructions to search for and destroy the enemy's ships and blockade their ports. Such measures would be less expensive than convoying American merchantmen with naval escorts. After some initial successes the war with Tripoli bogged down. Jefferson's opponents said "It is his war." They blamed the president for, in Jefferson's own words, sending "the *least* possible competent force." Excessive frugality had, in reality, prolonged the conflict and endangered American lives. Senator William Plumer of New Hampshire thought

it *bad policy, & base wickedness,* for a President to send brave men where they must inevitably be destroyed for the want of an adequate force. Had he sent a sufficient number of men & ships it would have been expensive—it might have endangered his reputation for economy & lessened his popularity with the rabble but would most probably have saved the lives of deserving men. He ought to have sent something more than a sufficiency—enough to inspire the men with confidence—to guard against accidents—& to insure success.[122]

By 1805 the pasha realized the war with America was counterproductive and he signed a peace treaty. Treaties were also signed with Algiers and Tunis. The United States was the only commercial nation whose ships could sail safely in the region without paying tribute.

A more serious diplomatic problem arose when in October 1802 Spain announced the closing of the port of New Orleans to American trade. Under President Washington, a treaty with Spain had formally opened the Mississippi River and the port of New Orleans to American navigation. Unbeknownst to Americans, Spain and France (now allies fighting Great Britain) had secretly agreed to transfer all of the Louisiana territory from Spanish to French control. Napoleon dreamed of recreating the French empire in the Western Hemisphere and the Spanish saw the French possession as an effective buffer separating Spain's lucrative Mexican colonies from the dangerous, ever-expanding American settlements. Jefferson viewed the transfer of Louisiana from a weak and ineffective Spanish rule to France as a danger. Writing to Robert R. Livingston, America's new minister to France, without the benefit of secret code, Jefferson indirectly let Napoleon know that a French acquisition of Louisiana would lead to an American alliance with Britain.

Jefferson then authorized Livingston to purchase New Orleans and West Florida for $10 million. As these diplomatic negotiations were transpiring, war fever raged in the American West and a grand French army sent to protect the new French holdings was decimated by rebel-

122. *Plumer's Memorandum*, December 31, 1804, pp. 234–35. Jefferson's actual words in his second annual address to Congress on December 15, 1802, were that "the smallest force competent" was sent "to secure our commerce in that sea."

lious slaves and fever in Santo Domingo. In need of money to carry on his European wars, Napoleon offered to sell America the entire Louisiana territory, stretching over 1,000 miles from the Mississippi River to the Rocky Mountains for $15 million. Uncertain of the constitutionality of buying territory from another country, Jefferson thought about seeking a constitutional amendment to authorize the purchase, but he realized that the opportunity had to be seized. He agreed to the purchase, creating for America an "empire for liberty." Minor opposition to the purchase arose in Congress, especially from New England Federalists who saw their region's relative strength in the Union weakened by such an immense acquisition of territory in which slavery might be permitted. The Senate ratified the treaty by a vote of 24 to 7. Already planning a scientific/military expedition to the Pacific Ocean, Jefferson now appointed his secretary Meriwether Lewis and William Clark to lead an indomitable corps of discovery across the continent.

With these major accomplishments, Jefferson was easily reelected. To avoid a repetition of the political and constitutional crisis posed by the election of 1800, the newly adopted Twelfth Amendment to the Constitution provided that candidates for president and vice president would run together as a ticket. With New York's elder statesman George Clinton replacing Aaron Burr as Jefferson's vice president, the Republican ticket resoundingly defeated the Federalist ticket of Charles Cotesworth Pinckney and Rufus King by an electoral vote of 162 to 14. Not only was Jefferson popular with the general public, but with Congress as well. Vermont Senator Stephen Roe Bradley said "That Mr. Jefferson's influence in Congress was irresistible—that it was alarming—That if he should recommend to us to repeal the Gospels of the Evangelist, a majority of Congress would do it."[123]

123. *Plumer's Memorandum*, December 11, 1806, p. 527.

When Jefferson's popularity was at its greatest and reelection was imminent, personal disaster struck. On April 17, 1804, Jefferson's younger daughter Polly died shortly after delivering her third child. With only Patsy surviving, Jefferson felt that he had "lost even the half of all I had."[124]

Jefferson's second administration was nearly as dismal as his first had been triumphal. As the European war intensified, both Britain and France preyed on American shipping. Wanting to avoid war at almost any cost, Jefferson and Secretary of State Madison used commerce as diplomatic leverage to moderate French and British naval aggression against neutral shipping. Nothing was achieved except economic hardship within America, large-scale smuggling of American goods outside of the country, and political opposition soaring to new heights in New England. Mathew Carey, a prominent Philadelphia printer, reported that had Jefferson been a Nero and Madison a Caligula, they could not have been "more completely abhorred & detested" than they were in New England.[125]

Shortly after his reelection Jefferson let it be known that he would not seek a third term. He would follow the two-term precedent set by Washington. Senator William Plumer considered this disclosure "as one of the most imprudent acts of Mr. Jefferson's public life."[126] As a lame-duck president, Jefferson lost political leverage, some of which was regained when several state legislatures and various private and public groups asked Jefferson to seek a third term. For a while Jefferson did nothing to suppress these overtures, but by 1807 he announced that he would not seek reelection. At this point he stepped back and refused to make decisions that would affect his successor.

124. To John Page, Washington, June 25, 1804, Washington, *Jefferson Writings*, IV, 547.

125. To James Madison, Philadelphia, August 12, 1812, *Madison Papers*, Pres. Ser., V, 149.

126. *Plumer's Memorandum*, March 16, 1806, p. 453.

His opponents said "the President wants nerve—he has not even confidence in himself . . . he has been in the habit of trusting almost implicitly in Mr. Madison. Madison has acquired a complete ascendancy over him."[127] Federalists also viewed Madison as "too cautious—too fearful & timid to direct the affairs of this nation," and many in the country agreed that there was no proper leadership. After Madison was elected president, Jefferson offered only opinion while the president-elect made all final decisions that Jefferson clothed "with the forms of authority."[128] In many ways, the last year of Jefferson's presidency was rudderless as the nation drifted between war and peace. Senator Plumer condemned the president. "Mr. Jefferson is too timid—too irresolute—too fickle—he wants nerve—he wants firmness & resolution. A wavering doubtful hesitating mind joined with credulity is oftentimes as injurious to the nation as a wicked depraved heart."[129]

RETIREMENT

Jefferson looked forward to retirement. On nearly the last day of his presidency, he wrote an old friend about retiring "to my family, my books & farms." Others would now be buffeted by political storms—he would not envy them. "Never," he wrote, "did a prisoner, released from his chains, feel such relief as I shall on shaking off the shackles of power. Nature intended me for the tranquil pursuits of science, by rendering them my supreme delight. But the enormities of the times in which I have lived, have forced me to take a part in resisting them, and to commit myself on the boisterous ocean of political passions."[130]

127. Ibid., April 8, 1806, p. 478.

128. Jefferson to James Monroe, Washington, January 28, 1809, Washington, *Jefferson Writings*, V, 420.

129. *Plumer's Memorandum*, March 16, 1806, p. 455.

130. To Pierre Samuel Dupont de Nemours, Washington, March 2, 1809, *Jefferson: Writings*, 1203.

Jefferson attended the inauguration of his successor, but tried to be as inconspicuous as possible, knowing that the day belonged to James Madison. After taking a week to settle his affairs and pack his belongings, Jefferson sent three wagons over land and a number of trunks via water to Monticello. He himself traveled by carriage until the roads became so "excessively bad" on the last three days that he rode on horseback alone—the final eight hours "through as disagreeable a snow storm as I was ever in."[131]

Patsy and her eight children greeted him. She and her husband lived on a neighboring plantation, but she regularly lived at Monticello when her father visited. She and her children would live at Monticello for the remaining seventeen years of Jefferson's life. Patsy would outlive her father by ten years.

Supervising his gardens and fields and rearing his grandchildren took up much of Jefferson's time. He established a large vegetable garden and enjoyed planting flowers and trees, the latter not for his own "gratification" but for "posterity."[132] "A Septuagenary," he wrote, "has no right to count on anything beyond annuals."[133] The former president loved trees. As secretary of state in Philadelphia his house was "entirely embosomed in high plane trees, with good grass below, & under them I breakfast, dine, write, read, & receive my company. What would I not give that the trees planted nearest round the house at Monticello were full grown."[134] While hosting one of his dinner parties as president, Jefferson exclaimed, "How I wish that I possessed the power of a despot." The guests sat astonished, before Jefferson finished his idea. "Yes, I wish I was a despot that I might save the noble, the beautiful trees that are daily falling sacrifices to the cupidity of

131. To James Madison, Monticello, March 17, 1809, Washington, *Jefferson Writings*, V, 437.

132. To Andrew Ellicott, Monticello, June 24, 1812, Jefferson Papers, Library of Congress.

133. To Samuel Brown, Monticello, April 17, 1813, ibid.

134. To Martha Jefferson, Philadelphia, July 7, 1793, ibid.

their owners, or the necessity of the poor."[135] Now that he was retired, he would replant trees on his own mountain.

Jefferson loved to work in the garden. If he were to relive his life

> It should have been on a rich spot of earth, well watered, and near a good market for the productions of the garden. No occupation is so delightful to me as the culture of the earth, & no culture comparable to that of the garden. Such a variety of subjects, some one always coming to perfection, the failure of one thing repaired by the success of another, & instead of one harvest, a continued one thro' the year. Under a total want of demand except for our family table. I am still devoted to the garden. But tho' an old man, I am but a young gardener.[136]

Visitors streamed into Monticello, many making the somewhat arduous three-day journey from Washington City. Perhaps typical was Margaret Bayard Smith and her husband William (editor of the influential Washington newspaper, the *National Intelligencer*), both close friends of the former president.[137] The Smiths arrived at Monticello on July 29, 1809, only five months after Jefferson had retired. After crossing the Rivanna, described by Mrs. Smith as "a wild & romantic little river," they wound their way up Jefferson's little mountain. The "untamed woodland," undeveloped by Jefferson's "superintending care" sur-

135. Margaret Bayard Smith, Reminiscences, Gaillard Hunt, ed., *The First Forty Years of Washington Society in the Family Letters of Margaret Bayard Smith* (New York, 1965, first printing 1906), 11.

136. To Charles Willson Peale, Poplar Forest, August 20, 1811, *Jefferson: Writings*, 1249.

137. For Margaret Bayard Smith's Account of her Visit to Monticello, July 29–August 1, 1809, see J. Jefferson Looney, ed., *The Papers of Thomas Jefferson* (Retirement Series, Princeton, 2004), I, 386–401.

prised Mrs. Smith. "Winding upwards" over a seemingly "endless road," they finally spied a corn field, but the road continued "wild & uncultivated." After two miles they reached the summit. Overcome with emotion, Mrs. Smith gazed upon the magnificent vista stretching for over sixty miles all around with the majestic "blue mountains, in all their grandeur." As their carriage approached the house, Jefferson appeared on horseback returning from his "morning ride." He welcomed the Smiths and brought them through the main hall of the manor house into a drawing room where they relaxed and enjoyed refreshments with Jefferson and his daughter Patsy (Mrs. Thomas Mann Randolph).

At 5:00 P.M. the first of two bells rang calling the family and guests to assemble for dinner. The second bell signaled that seats should be taken at the cloth-covered table as dinner was ready to be served. The Smiths joined a dozen family members that included Jefferson, his daughter and son-in-law, Jefferson's grandchildren (eventually there would be a dozen), and a young man resident at Monticello studying law with Jefferson. "The table was plainly, but genteely & plentifully spread." Jefferson's French and Italian wines were followed by Madeira and "a sweet ladies wine." After dessert, the company stayed seated in conversation. Because Jefferson withdrew after breakfast either to his chambers for writing or riding throughout the plantation, this after dinnertime was reserved for the family. After the dinnertime conversations ended, the company separated and some took walks throughout the maze of mountaintop roads and pathways. They passed by Jefferson's vegetable garden which was not yet completely established. It consisted of a plot of leveled land terraced on the south side of the mountain stretching 800 by 40 feet. A second similarly-sized terraced garden was scheduled to be erected slightly below the first one. After the walk, the adults reconvened in a drawing room where at 9:00 P.M. tea and fruit were served. Jefferson usually retired after the tea, not partaking of the fruit. The rest of the company usually retired within an hour.

Mrs. Smith awakened early the next morning to view the sunrise. She gazed down upon a vast ocean of fog punctured only intermittently by the tops of forested mountains looking like islands. As the sun baked off the fog, lakes, bays, and rivers appeared. Often the morning was tinctured with showers or mists during which the clouds threw off large masses of shade onto the mountains interspersed with a variety of spots shaped by the sunshine. Rainbows often plunged downward to the river 500 feet below. On rare occasions a moonlight rainbow appeared. Like dinner, breakfast was announced with two bells and consisted of tea, coffee, muffins, wheat and corn bread, butter, and cold ham. After breakfast the family dispersed. Jefferson "went to his apartments, the door of which is never opened but by himself." The seclusion seemed so sacred that Mrs. Smith told Jefferson "it was his sanctum sanctorum." Jefferson's son-in-law left to ride over to his plantation, not usually returning till the evening. Mr. Bankhead, the law student, went off to his study in an adjoining building, while Jefferson Randolph (Jefferson's grandson) left to survey a tract of woodland. Mrs. Randolph took her children to the nursery where she cared for them. She also served as their tutor when not occupied with the supervision of the house-keeping chores. After breakfast visitors either retired to their rooms or took walks or rides throughout the grounds. Those who read filled their time with books from Jefferson's extensive library. Then, between 4:00 P.M. and 5:00 P.M., the dinner bells would ring again.

As each year passed Jefferson noticed various faculties diminishing. "Last year it was the sight, this it is the hearing, the next something else will be going, until all is gone."[138] He began wearing spectacles at night and when reading small print during the day. His hearing in a group gave him difficulty. He had a little rheumatism in his left hip and the aching in his wrists caused by dislocations many years before made his writing slow and painful. But fortunately he retained good health, which he ascribed partly to his temperate living: diet—primarily vegetarian; drink—coffee or tea for breakfast; wine, beer, malt liquor, and cider at other times, but never ardent spirits; exercise—walking a mile winded him but riding a horse six to eight miles a day (and sometimes thirty to forty miles) invigorated him; and partly to a sixty-year ritual of bathing his feet in cold water every morning. In an age of poor dental care, he was proud that he had lost no teeth to age. He slept five to eight hours nightly, "according as my company or the book I am reading interests me." No matter how many hours he slept, he rose with the sun.[139]

Jefferson found "delight" in corresponding with old and intimate friends, especially Benjamin Rush, and with John Adams with whom Rush arranged a reconciliation in 1812. On hearing that the two friends had started corresponding, Rush wrote Adams that "I rejoice in the correspondence which has taken place between you and your old friend Mr. Jefferson. I consider you and him as the North and South Poles of the American Revolution. Some talked, some wrote, and some fought to promote and establish it, but you and Mr. Jefferson *thought* for us all."[140]

Adams tended to write three letters to Jefferson for every one he received from him. But if Jefferson enjoyed writing to friends, the great burden of his retirement was

138. To William Duane, Monticello, October 1, 1812, Washington, *Jefferson Writings*, VI, 80.

139. Most of the information in this paragraph comes from Jefferson's letter to Vine Utley, Monticello, March 21, 1819, *Jefferson: Writings*, 1416–17.

140. Rush to Adams, Philadelphia, February 17, 1812, L. H. Butterfield, ed., *Letters of Benjamin Rush* (2 vols., Princeton, 1951), II, 1127.

answering the hundreds of letters from strangers who wrote "civilly" and made it "hard to refuse them civil answers."[141] Although this "drudgery of the writing table" denied him the pleasure of reading as much as he would like, yet he still made it a point never to "go to bed without an hour, or half hour's previous reading of something moral, whereon to ruminate in the intervals of sleep."[142]

One of the happiest and yet saddest events in Jefferson's life occurred in 1815. After the British burned the Capitol building in Washington during the dark days of the War of 1812, Jefferson offered to replace Congress' library with his own for whatever Congress was willing to pay. He had spent fifty years gathering his magnificent collection of 6,500 volumes. He had "spared no pains, no opportunity or expense, to make it what it is." He had spent his free afternoons in Paris searching the bookstores and he had standing orders at the "principal book-marts" in the major cities of Europe. He acquired "everything which related to America, and indeed whatever was rare and valuable in every science." Most of the volumes were well bound; many elegantly so. It was quite simply, a literary treasure.[143] Congress paid $23,000 for the library. Ten wagons hauled the books away nailed shut in Jefferson's original bookcases. Jefferson immediately felt the emptiness, the void in Monticello, and unable to restrain himself, Jefferson started to acquire another library. "I cannot live without books," he told John Adams. He would need fewer now; only those necessary for his own "amusement."[144]

Throughout his life, Jefferson wanted to reform education in Virginia. In retirement he again considered the

141. To John Adams, Monticello, January 11, 1817, *Adams-Jefferson Letters*, 505.

142. To Vine Utley, Monticello, March 21, 1819, *Jefferson: Writings*, 1417.

143. To Samuel H. Smith, Monticello, September 21, 1814, ibid., 1353–54.

144. To John Adams, Monticello, June 10, 1815, *Adams-Jefferson Letters*, 443.

problem and decided to propose something that might be attainable—a publicly supported university. Georgia and North and South Carolina had already established such universities. Jefferson obtained a charter from the state legislature, selected the site, served on the board of visitors and as the first rector, raised the necessary public and private funds, drafted the curriculum, recruited the faculty, designed the plan of the academic village, and drew the architectural plans for the buildings, including the Rotunda, the grand central building modeled after the Pantheon in Rome. About a year before Jefferson's death, after more than a decade of hard work, the University of Virginia opened with its first class of about thirty students.

In December 1824, Daniel Webster spent five days visiting Jefferson at Monticello. Webster took extensive notes describing his remarkable host and their conversations on a myriad of topics.

> Mr. Jefferson is between 81 & 82—over 6 ft. high—an ample long frame—rather thin & spare. His head which is not peculiar in its shape is set rather forward upon his shoulders & his neck being long when he is in conversation, or walking, there is a considerable protrusion of his chin.—His head is still well covered with hair, which having been once red & now turning to white, is of an indistinct, light, sandy colour— His eyes are small, & very light & now, neither striking, nor brilliant—His chin is rather long & not sharp. His teeth are still good. His mouth well formed & generally compressed with an expression of benevolence & contentment. His skin formerly light, and freckled, is now rough & bears the marks of age & cutaneous affections. His limbs are uncommonly long & his wrists of extraordinary size. His walk is not precise & mil-

itary, but easy & swinging. He stoops a little, not
so much from age, as from constitutional formation—When sitting he seems short & low, partly
from not sitting erect & partly from the dispro-
portionate length of his limbs. He wears a dark
grey surtout coat—a yellow kersimere waist coat,
with an under one faced with a dingy red. His
pantaloons are very loose, long & of the same
material with his coat. His hose are grey woolen
& his shoes those which bear his name. His
whole dress not slovenly, but neglected. He wears
a common round hat & when he rides on horseback, a grey strait bodiced coat, & a long spencer
of the same material both fastened with pearl
buttons. When we first saw him riding, he wore
round his neck, instead of a cravat, a white
woolen tippet & to guard his feet, black velvet
gaiters under his pantaloons. His general appearance indicated an extraordinary degree of health,
vivacity & spirits for his age. His sight is still
good, as he needs spectacles only in the evening.
His hearing is not much impaired, but a number
of voices in animated conversation around him,
seems to confound it.

He rises in the morning, as soon as he can see
the hands of his clock & examines his thermome-
ter immediately, for he keeps a regular meteoro-
logical diary. Until breakfast, he employs himself
chiefly in writing. He breakfasts at nine. From
that hour till dinner, he is employed in his study;
excepting that on every fair day he rides from 7 to
14 miles on horseback. He dines at 4; retires to
the drawing room about 6, passes the succeeding
hours in conversation & goes to bed at nine—His
habit of retiring early is so strong that it has
become essential to his health. His breakfast is
made up of tea & coffee & bread in all the good

Virginia varieties of which he does not seem afraid however new & warm. He enjoys his dinner well, taking with his food a large proportion of vegetables. With regard to wine, he may be said to excell both in the knowledge & the use— His preference is for wines of the continent of which he has many sorts of excellent quality. His dinners are in the half French, half Virginia style, in good taste & abundant. No wine served before the cloth is removed. Tea & coffee in the saloon between 7 & 8—His conversation is easy & natural & apparently not ambitious—It is not loud as challenging general attention, but usually address[ed] to the person next to him—The topics, when not selected with regard to the character & feelings of his auditors, are those subjects with which his mind seems now particularly occupied. And these at present may be justly said to be first science & letters & especially the University of Virginia, which will rise it is to be hoped to usefulness & credit under his continued care. When we were with him, his favorite literary subjects were Greek & Anglo-Saxon, & secondly historical recollections of the times of the Revolution & of his residence in France, from 1783 to 89.[145]

As Jefferson got old, he experienced the pain of seeing friends die. Jefferson wondered whether it was desirable "to witness the death of all our companions, and merely be the last victim?" He doubted it. Why he asked,

145. Notes of Mr. Jefferson's Conversation 1824 at Monticello, Jefferson Papers, University of Virginia. Dated December 1825. A slightly different copy is in the New Hampshire Historical Society and published in Charles M. Wiltse and Harold D. Moser, eds., *The Papers of Daniel Webster*, Correspondence (4 vols., Hanover, N.H., 1974–1980), I, 370–71.

would one choose to remain "as a solitary trunk in a desolate field, from which all its former companions have disappeared?"[146] But the survivors have "the traveller's consolation. Every step shortens the distance we have to go; the end of our journey is in sight."[147] He wrote to John Adams that "There is a ripeness of time for death, regarding others as well as ourselves, when it is reasonable we should drop off, and make room for another growth. When we have lived our generation out, we should not wish to encroach on another."[148]

When Abigail Adams died in 1818, Jefferson wrote his old friend John Adams a letter of condolence, as someone who had lost a beloved wife and children.

> Tried myself, in the school of affliction, by the loss of every form of connection which can rive the human heart, I know well, and feel what you have lost, what you have suffered, are suffering, and have yet to endure. The same trials have taught me that, for ills so immeasurable, time and silence are the only medicines. I will not therefore, by useless condolences, open afresh the sluices of your grief nor, altho' mingling sincerely my tears with yours, will I say a word more, where words are vain, but that it is of some comfort to us both that the term is not very distant at which we are to deposit, in the same cerement, our sorrows and suffering bodies, and to ascend in essence to an ecstatic meeting with the friends we have loved and lost and whom we shall still love and never lose again. God bless you and support you under your heavy affliction.[149]

146. To Maria Cosway, Monticello, December 27, 1820, Jefferson Papers, Massachusetts Historical Society.

147. To John Page, Washington, June 25, 1804, Washington, *Jefferson Writings*, IV, 547.

148. Monticello, August 1, 1816, *Adams-Jefferson Letters*, 484.

149. Monticello, November 13, 1818, ibid., 529.

Two years later, facing their own mortality, Jefferson again wrote Adams.

> We . . . have done for our country the good which has fallen in our way, so far as commensurate with the faculties given us. That we have not done more than we could cannot be imputed to us as a crime before any tribunal. I look therefore to that crisis, as I am sure you also do, as one "qui summum nec metuit diem nec optat" [who neither fears the final day nor hopes for it].[150]

In one of the great unbelievable coincidences of history, Jefferson and Adams both died only hours apart on July 4, 1826—the fiftieth anniversary of the Declaration of Independence. Recognizing the importance of the symbolism for the new country, both men valiantly held on to life until that glorious anniversary arrived. It was their final gift to a grateful country. On hearing of Jefferson's death, James Madison, Jefferson's friend for fifty years, wrote that "he lives and will live in the memory and gratitude of the wise & good, as a luminary of Science, as a votary of liberty, as a model of patriotism, and as a benefactor of the human kind."[151]

150. Monticello, March 14, 1820, ibid., 562–63.
151. To Nicholas P. Trist, Montpelier, July 6, 1826, Jack N. Rakove, ed., *James Madison: Writings* (New York, 1999), 812.

BIBLIOGRAPHY

Boyd, Julian P. et al., eds. *The Papers of Thomas Jefferson.* Princeton, 1950–. Cited as *Jefferson Papers.*

Brown, Everett Somerville, ed. *William Plumer's Memorandum of Proceedings in the Senate, 1803–1807.* New York, 1923. Cited as *Plumer's Memorandum.*

Butterfield, L. H. et al., eds. *Adams Family Correspondence.* Cambridge, Mass., 1963–.

Butterfield, L. H., ed. *Letters of Benjamin Rush.* 2 vols. Princeton, 1951.

Butterfield, L. H. et al., eds. *Diary and Autobiography of John Adams.* 4 vols. Cambridge, Mass., 1962.

Cappon, Lester J., ed. *The Adams-Jefferson Letters: The Complete Correspondence Between Thomas Jefferson and Abigail and John Adams.* Chapel Hill, N.C., 1959. Cited as *Adams-Jefferson Letters.*

Hunt, Gaillard, ed. *The First Forty Years of Washington Society in the Family Letters of Margaret Bayard Smith.* New York, 1965, first printing 1906.

Hutchinson, William T. et al., eds. *The Papers of James Madison.* Chicago and Charlottesville, 1962–. Cited as *Madison Papers.*

Idzerda, Stanley J. et al., eds. *Lafayette in the Age of the American Revolution: Selected Letters and Papers, 1776–1790.* 5 vols. Ithaca, N.Y., 1977–1983.

Jackson, Donald et al., eds., *The Papers of George Washington.* Charlottesville, Va., 1976–. Cited as *Washington Papers.*

Jefferson Papers, Library of Congress.

Jefferson Papers, University of Virginia.

Johnson, Herbert A. et al., eds. *The Papers of John Marshall.* Williamsburg, Va., 1974–.

Kaminski, John P., ed. *A Necessary Evil?: Slavery and the Debate Over the Constitution.* Madison, Wis., 1995.

Kaminski, John P., ed. *Jefferson in Love: The Love Letters between Thomas Jefferson & Maria Cosway.* Madison, Wis., 1999.

Kline, Mary-Jo, ed. *Political Correspondence and Public Papers of Aaron Burr.* 2 vols. Princeton, 1983.

"Dr. Mitchill's Letters from Washington: 1801–1813." *Harper's New Monthly Magazine,* 58 (1879).

Peterson, Merrill D., ed. *Thomas Jefferson: Writings.* New York, 1984. Cited as *Jefferson: Writings.*

Risjord, Norman K. *Thomas Jefferson.* Madison, Wis., 1994.

Schutz, John A. and Douglas Adair, eds. *The Spur of Fame: Dialogues of John Adams and Benjamin Rush, 1805–1813,* reprint ed., Indianapolis, n.d.

Smith, Paul H., ed. *Letters of Delegates to Congress, 1774–1789.* 26 vols. Washington, D.C., 1976–2000. Cited as Smith, *Letters.*

Story, William W., ed. *Life and Letters of Joseph Story.* 2 vols. Boston, 1851.

Syrett, Harold C., ed. *The Papers of Alexander Hamilton.* 27 vols. New York, 1961–1987. Cited as *Hamilton Papers.*

Washington, H. A., ed. *The Writings of Thomas Jefferson.* 9 vols. Washington, D.C., 1853–1854. Cited as Washington, *Jefferson Writings.*

Wiltse, Charles M., and Harold D. Moser, eds. *The Papers of Daniel Webster,* Correspondence. 4 vols. Hanover, N.H., 1974–1980.

Transcription Policy

The transcription policies of different documentary editions have varied over the years. I have relied on the text in the printed volumes cited in this bibliography with one exception. Whenever possible I have checked and used a literal transcription of the original manuscript of Jefferson's letters.